CUT

INSIDE THE RESTAURANT BUSINESS

Andrew Parkinson is head chef at Bertorelli's,
Charlotte Street, Fitzrovia, London.

Jonathon Green's many books include *Days in the Life*,
All Dressed Up and *The Cassell Dictionary of Slang*.

CUTTING IT FINE

INSIDE THE RESTAURANT BUSINESS

Andrew Parkinson

with

Jonathon Green

VINTAGE

Published by Vintage 2002

2 4 6 8 10 9 7 5 3 1

Text copyright © Andrew Parkinson and Jonathon Green 2001

Andrew Parkinson and Jonathon Green have asserted their
rights under the Copyright, Designs and Patents Act 1988 to
be identified as the author of this work

First published in Great Britain in 2001 by Jonathan Cape

Vintage
Random House, 20 Vauxhall Bridge Road,
London SW1V 2SA

Random House Australia (Pty) Limited
20 Alfred Street, Milsons Point, Sydney,
New South Wales 2061, Australia

Random House New Zealand Limited
18 Poland Road, Glenfield,
Auckland 10, New Zealand

Random House (Pty) Limited
Endulini, 5A Jubilee Road, Parktown 2193,
South Africa

The Random House Group Limited Reg. No. 954009
www.randomhouse.co.uk

A CIP catalogue record for this book is available from the British Library

ISBN 0 09 928372 7

Papers used by Random House Group Limited are natural,
recyclable products made from wood grown in sustainable forests.
The manufacturing processes conform to the environmental
regulations of the country of origin

Printed and bound in Great Britain by
Cox & Wyman Ltd, Reading, Berkshire

CONTENTS

One day in 1987, after a day studying food at Perth College, I decided to try to write about what it was like working as a commis chef at the five-star Gleneagles Hotel. I wanted to try to capture the hectic, high-pressure environment of the hotel kitchen and the mental toughness of the brigade of chefs who worked there.

That piece was never written, but now, fourteen years later, having worked in a variety of other kitchens, that youthful daydream has become reality in the form of the book you are about to read. In 1998 I was approached by Jonathon Green, who asked me if I would co-operate on a book about the day-to-day operations of a busy kitchen in a London restaurant, about the reality of the restaurant business as I saw it. I met Jonathon through his son Lucien, who is also a chef. We agreed to write a book together.

Our journey through the next two and a half years

has been a colourful one. We have spent exhausting nights in the bitter cold traipsing round meat, fish and vegetable markets. Jonathon would arrive at the restaurant before sunrise to watch the first deliveries of the day, and then return in the evening to witness the hectic evening service – and, on a good day, to witness the customer enjoy the food we have cooked for him.

Everything in this book is written from my own personal experience. I do not claim to be a Michelin-star chef, though I admire enormously everything that such chefs achieve and the dedication it takes to reach such a level. Such people are rare, however. Most chefs are like me, and work in kitchens like mine, and it is this reality that I hope we have captured in *Cutting It Fine*.

Andrew Parkinson

PREFACE

Monday morning. Seven a.m. The restaurant's been shut since the end of Saturday night service. It's a new week. Everything's coming in from the suppliers — meat, fish and vegetables. Stuff we ordered last thing Saturday night. We're going to be really busy and there's a shitload of work to do. So I've got a lot of prep to do this morning. Which is good, gives you an adrenalin rush. You've got to get it done as quickly as possible, as the time flies by. The only bonus on a Monday is that at least you don't expect to be busy on lunches. There'll be bookings, but in a way I don't really care what they are — I know I've got a lot of meat and fish coming in anyway and that'll cover us for today. The most important thing is getting myself sorted out . . .

I live in Essex, which means I've been up since quarter past five this morning, that's normal. I walk out the house at twenty to six, walk up the road, get a bus and get to Romford station at six minutes to six. I get off at Stratford, go to Tottenham Court Road, then walk up into Soho. Soho isn't the freshest-smelling place in the mornings as I walk to work; the sooner I'm in the kitchen the better.

The first thing I've got to do is the stock-take: I do it on a Monday morning before everybody gets in. We've got to write down the weights of everything. I check it off on lists, which are based on what is on the menu. When we change things on the menu, this will all change and new stuff gets put in.

The stock-take's never going to be 100 per cent accurate, maybe 95 per cent. Chefs think they can fiddle it, but there's no way you can. If you fiddle it this week, it'll come back on you next week. Then it's the chef's fault for being stupid. Every week we write down how much we've got in stock today. Come next week you can't fiddle it because when it's totalled up against what we've sold, it might work out completely different. What you have to remember is that if you buy in 350 onglets this week and sell 300, you should obviously have fifty left and they should be accounted for. If you can't account for them questions will be asked. Why would you want to fiddle? Well, people try it. Gives them a better bonus. They can make cash out of it. The best way to keep your stock control as tight as possible is to keep your ordering as low as you think sensible on the Saturday, having only what you think is enough food in the building to see you through to the end of the night. This means that, come Monday, you're not carrying too much stock. It's a bit of a gamble: the last thing you want is for the first forty customers to order fillet steak and then run out by eight p.m.

It's an informed gamble, though – I've been doing this for years now.

In the upstairs kitchen we've got two walk-in fridges – one is the meat, fish and garnish fridge, the other dairy, fruit and veg. You can't have eggs in the same fridge as your milk; someone from health and safety said we couldn't. Totally bemuses me. Anyway, that's what we've got to do. So we had to move the eggs to the meat and fish fridge. Can't understand why.

It gets very cold in a fridge, so we do this stock-take as quickly as possible. We used to do it at the end of service on a Saturday night, so we had to wait until the very last check went out. It was changed as company policy. They bought three new restaurants, which closed on a Sunday, so they decided the entire group's stock-taking should coincide with theirs. Twenty-three restaurants had to change their way of doing things for just three restaurants.

In the fridges all the containers have got labels on them: what the product is, which chef made it, the date it was made and the use-by date. This is another health and safety must. It also helps to ensure that, if one of the chefs has made something poorly, I'll know exactly who did it. You can also use a colour-coded daily system, i.e. red labels for Monday, blue for Tuesday, green for Wednesday, and so on. This works if all you need to know is the day the food was made, but there's no room for the other details I want to know. So it's no use to me.

Once we've written down all the stock, the amount of each is put into the computer; every item already having its current price per kilo on file. So, if you've got two kilos of sirloin in stock, the computer will automatically add that up, and so on for all the other items. This way, once everything's been fed into the computer, it'll tell you the final value of the stock-take. We work out how much money we spent last week on food, then how much we made on food, and that gives us our profit and loss. A big restaurant, say Quaglino's, might spend £25,000 a week on its raw materials. For us it's between £6,000 and £7,000. At the end of every week all the invoices have to be put through the computer – company name, invoice number, amount – then the computer adds it all up. That's where you get your weekly spend from. It's an administrator's job to do that, but ours has been off ill, so I decided that the sous chef and I would do it ourselves. You've also got to check every invoice that goes through. I'm in a business now where, although I'm cooking, I've got to make money for the company. Before I became a head chef I didn't understand that as I do now . . . you did loads of hours, worked really hard and got your pay packet . . . but that was as far as you went.

Stock means new, unopened. If something's been opened and used, you can't class it as stock. It's got to be full. You don't always have to weigh everything, just average it out. If I've got two boxes more or less the same size, then I weigh one of them. You get used to an average weight for everything you've got. No point in weighing each lemon. Just count them: we get a hundred lemons in a box and so we divide the price of the box by one hundred. Simple. There's short cuts: we know what we've got, what the containers hold. If we've got a full container of, say, carrots, it's the same as the bag of carrots we get from the supplier.

So. The dairy. We got the milk right. Didn't get the cream right. Too much left. One loaf of Sunblest – for the *croque-monsieurs* downstairs, and the odd chef's sandwich. We've got the egg yolks spot on, liquid eggs: spot on. Emmental: spot on. We've done really well this week. In other words, last week we ordered accurately. What we want is to find that we've nearly run out come the end of Saturday night. Yeah, we do, we want it that tight. If we keep it really tight this week, we've got to do the same next week. If we don't keep it tight, when we get to next week it'll look as if we've over-ordered. Ideally there's no waste, nothing gets thrown out. If we keep to daily ordering, the control's better.

Lots of foie gras, butter — we use about five boxes a week, for *béarnaise*, sauces, cooking and the restaurants — truffle dressing, tomato vinaigrette, *beurre blanc*. I've got tomato juice. I've hardly got any meat in. I've got some venison here, which is from the end of last week, weighs 2.5 kilos. But I can use that this week: it's been marinaded. I've got no bacon, no beef fillets, no calves' feet. I've actually got calves' liver. I've got 1.8 kilos of calves' liver. Caul fat, I've got 250 grams. Use it for wrapping kidneys. Chicken breasts, four left. Chicken livers, no. Smoked chicken, no. Chicken whole, no. We must have sold thirty-four chickens on Saturday night. Sold a lot anyway. Duck breasts, no. French ham, 5 kilos. There's no piglet left. What this means is that I should be shitting myself because it means we've got nothing in stock really, but the butcher gets here in an hour and the fridges will be topped up again.

I've got a shitload of meat coming in. Quite a fair bit of fish, loads of veg. This butter we're getting, I know as head chef what we should be getting in and what we've got in here. So, for instance, we've got three boxes of butter. What'll happen at the end of the week is that we'll end up with one box of butter and probably no clarified whatever. Really, these suppliers don't want you to order little minimums, but because I know we've got two boxes of clarified in there, we won't use that this week. We'll probably need one more box of butter, so I'll have to get another box at the end of the week now. It would have been better if I'd just ordered no clarified and three boxes of butter, and then on, say, Friday I could have got one box and three clarified, and made it worth it for the supplier to come out.

We have got dried stores that we stock-take as well, but dry stores are done on a Sunday evening very kindly by the pastry chefs. So after the meat fridge it's the fish. Just mark up which fish we've got. This is prep stuff, ready for all sections, so they keep themselves *en place* (that is, with food prepared and ready to cook). Good, we've done really well again. We've got 6 kilos of salmon *en place*, which isn't bad. We've got no smoked salmon. Mussels, we've got. Monkfish . . .

I've also got to check the Rôtisserie fridges, which are downstairs. Same process. Except there the restaurant's open seven days every week. We need to count here too. Back to the meat again, box of steaks. We've got 5 kilos of sirloin . . . twenty onglets in packs of ten – that's a French cut of steak. The onglet cut comes from underneath a sirloin, between the sirloin and the fillet – if I'm correct. Just this little piece of meat, a tiny fillet. That's an onglet. They split it down, bash it up and make money on it. Obviously from a big animal. We use about 300 a week, maybe 350. And that's just us. Cows get slaughtered every day, just for this . . . And I see there I've got some more salmon. So that's now going to be . . . 8 kilos of salmon in stock. A bit bad. Then the dairy. Eight trays of eggs . . . liquid eggs. There's one times 5 litres. No, that's it, all the fish we've got. That's it. And the pastry chef will tell me how much pastry and ice-cream he's got left.

That's my stock-take done. It's twenty past seven and I'm rocking. Now it's back to work.

First thing now is to get the stoves going, have them ready for when the chefs start arriving. Today I've got a *mise en place* list to get together, got to do all the prep ready for service again, ready to start again Monday morning — bang. That's what it's all about. Half the staff come in looking like shit — they've been on the piss all weekend. Oh, they're all nice lads. But they don't go out like we used to. A Monday morning at Odette's, where I used to work, was just a nightmare. If you didn't eat before you started work, the more you went on the more ill you felt — all that food. Then you'd have to start scaling all your fish . . . I always felt like shit on a Monday morning at Odette's — guaranteed.

The blast chiller has to be checked every morning — things are put in there overnight. When I do go through it, I find that the night before chefs have kept potatoes and veg back; from parties or from the service, and put it in there thinking we can use it the next night. But you can't really, so I just bin it or give it to the staff.

With all the deliveries coming there's an incredible amount being done simultaneously in a very short time. In another kitchen the head chef might not do this, but I prefer it this way. Unpacking the meat and fish isn't that complex, but like every-thing else you can do it right or wrong. One of the boys was doing it last week. Doing the meat and fish — it was as much as we got today — but he was still doing it at two p.m. That proves to him it's not an easy job. If you're gonna do it, you gotta get it done quick, precisely, and out of the way. But he messed around, had a bit of a stroll. Anyway, it pissed me off. I told him, one day chef, I'm gonna leave you to run the kitchen for two days. You're gonna need to be on the middle of the pass at twelve o'clock because we're so busy and you don't want to be doing the unpacking at two p.m. So sort yourself out.

I mean obviously you try and keep the back of the kitchen as tidy as possible and put everything away as fast as you can, but it does build up. There's this sign on the stairway outside the kitchen back door saying, 'The Stairway and Exit Way to be kept clear of goods, bins, rubbish and obstructions', but the fact is that now, though it won't be for long, there are a number of empty boxes out there, two very large pots full of pigs' trotters, chicken carcasses, various other things to make stock, a large box of salad and two big boxes of pre-cut chips, one large box of onions, one large box of shallots and two large polythene bags of potatoes. It's all got to be dealt with and it really shouldn't be on the stairway but, hey, it's Christmas.

All the meat's coming in now. The drivers get to their place around three in the morning and start loading up. All the restaurants have sent in their orders and the drivers have their separate runs. I think our supplier has around twenty. All over London. The vans actually come out about four or five times a day, but I don't really want that because it gives me more invoices. That's why I try and order once a day only. But sometimes you forget something and you have to order twice.

Look what I've got today: sirloins, fillets, veal bones, calves' feet, chicken bones, smoked chickens, whole chickens, chicken livers, pork, onglets, English lamb, lamb shanks, bacon, Parma ham, sirloin, beef fillet . . . chickens . . . kidneys . . . pigs' trotters and chicken carcasses for the stock. All fillets are wrapped in peach paper. It sops up all the blood. It's very thin, works out at about one penny per sheet. Something I'd never seen till I worked in a big restaurant a few years back. This is a lot of meat, around £500 worth.

So now I need to get all the shit out of the way as quickly as possible because everyone'll start falling over the food soon. The quicker you do this the better, but you realise you've got to work at speed to get this in the fridge.

All these shanks, they're all cut to spec . . . With chickens, we get a 4lb chicken, and with that he'll bone it, give us the breasts – which means we've got to get big ones – then we get the carcasses to use for stock. A 4lb chicken costs us about £3 a bird. Very good value. I'm not going to tell you how much we make on 'em. For what it's worth I think we're too cheap. That's two boxes of chicken done. It's ten past nine. So it's going to take an hour to put away. Now I've got fillets and kidneys . . . That's a whole fillet. You take about six or seven portions out of it. That will be *châteaubriand*. Have to wrap it quite tightly in clingfilm, you wrap it first, then you slice it. It keeps its shape that way . . . If it's too long, you can cut it into strips, for *plat du jour*. Kidneys now. Most of the time the kidneys are quite large, a two-portion size, but I wrap them up individually. Then when we get an order we can cook them individually. I made a mistake when I was somewhere else, wrapping them up together, or wrapping the whole lot up – too much waste. These are duck legs for *confit*. First you put them in a sort of dry marinade, some garlic, sea salt. I've got sea salt on it, garlic, thyme, rosemary. Just leave it in this box, clingfilm over it, for about forty-eight hours. What you don't want to do is cover it with sea salt and leave it for too long. Then it'd be really salty. Then it's bang into the fridge . . . When we get fillets in, we also get the mince. It's the offcuts minced up. Which means that it's effectively free. These are my sirloins. I ordered two, and I can get around twenty-two cuts off each one. The butcher's cut all these for me. I put them back in these plastic containers, covered with the peach paper. This is a leg of lamb; the butcher bones it for me. It's got three segments on it, and they cut it into the three segments and roll it out and tie them. I'll marinade them now in oil, lemon juice and salt.

9

Ten minutes to ten and the meat's done. £500 worth unwrapped, parcelled up, put away — dealt with . . .

At the same time everyone else is getting on with their job. Albert, who's the chief kitchen porter [KP], is dealing with salads. Looking at the stoves now, I can see stock cooking, six large pans: one flat pan, two frying pans. As you can see, they're all busy cooking away. It's the same for each section of the kitchen — fish, sauce, larder — Monday morning and no *mise en place*: so everyone's chasing the clock. Two frying pans cooking mushrooms. Potatoes cooking in a large pan . . . When they're ready another KP is going to be putting them through a mashing machine. We're also getting the chips ready in the fryer. We need to blanch them three-quarters of the way while the fryer's low, then they go into the blast chiller. When it comes to service time, whack 'em back in to crisp on the outside. *Mise en place* is always a morning job. We're doing it now, but come the evening it'll be stowed away and the only thing we'll be doing is using it for dishes.

The veg man's fucked up. He's just dumped it all and fucked off and I haven't checked it. I could ring up and say, 'We're missing this, this and this.' They'll say, 'Oh, we sent it,' but I couldn't check that, the driver pissed off. The driver's gonna get into trouble. Just left everything outside the back door. Pisses me off, coming later and later all the time. I said, 'You've got to get here earlier.' So he did and got here so early that the place was still locked up — so he dumped it all outside the restaurant in the street. A few years ago I had a shitty time with an old veg supplier who was giving me delivery problems. One day I just took it all in, then rang up and asked where my delivery was.

You've got to check the prices, everything's going up by a

pound here, a pound there. This is supposed to be a kilo of dried ceps, costs £34. I don't think that's a kilo. And he's charged me for a kilo, so I'd better ring him up now . . . I've got one more veg supplier to come in now . . . Peppers and herbs. I do check the weights. These green beans, they don't look like a kilo, but they are. Still, it's worth checking.

Another veg supplier just rang me up and asked me why he hadn't got an order on a Monday morning. He has it now, any-way. I don't know why – the sous chef never put the order through. Things like this happen. It won't screw me up because he might have delivered about now. Now it'll be another hour or so. I don't use him for much and he always thinks there's some-thing wrong if I don't take anything off him. They worry about things like that. Then, if you ring up to order, they'll say, 'Oh, I'm really busy, OK?' But the other day I rang up and hung on and hung on and hung on. Tough, man . . . That really pissed me off and I just put the phone down. There's always a few problems like that. Put your order through, it doesn't turn up right. The fish supplier says he hasn't got this or this. Slam the phone down. Here we go again. Your fillets are supposed to be 7–8 oz, they come in at 5 oz. On and on and on, all through the day.

It's ten-fifteen. Here's the fish. About £360 worth. Good-quality fish was always better on a Tuesday. But our supplier, everything's top-class, they refrigerate it really well, so even on a Monday you don't have to worry about getting off fish. Smoked haddock – very nice. Right, so you start cleaning the fish at quarter past ten . . . £360 worth of fish, mainly very large salmon. Six sides. I have a spec for the salmon – it needs to be a big fish – the whole fish a lot wider, bigger belly, and it means I can get a better cut for an escalope. With the salmon, he's charging a little bit more because I'm getting bigger fish. But he was sending me in smaller fish now and again and still charging the same price. So I rang up the other day and said, 'If I don't get the salmon I asked for, I'll get if off someone else.' That would mean him losing a thirty salmon order every week. If you let them rule you, they'll get away with anything. The first thing to do is prep up this salmon. What I'll do, got lots of bones here, so . . . take the bones out . . . If you get the bones out the way, then just take the fish off there. All these trimmings I put into fish-cakes. 110 grams . . . Fuck me, I'm miles out. So this one's gonna be 170–180 grams. This will be sent downstairs. It can go on the grill, cook *à la minute*. A cheaper cut and you get more portions out of one fish if you do it this way. And because we cut it on an angle it sort of deceives in a way . . . They think they are getting a big portion, getting their money's worth. It's not what I'd call deliberate deceit – just business. This is called weaverfish. You can sting yourself on it when you cut it. It's got poisonous spikes. There was a fella killed on holiday in Greece, or Algeria, by one. We don't fillet the plaice, we serve it on the bone. Just take the skin off the mouth, all this here. Last thing's swordfish. Sell a lot of swordfish. The trimmings I use as *salade niçoise* down-stairs. Swordfish and tuna.

And that's it. All this started about twenty-past eight and it's now three hours later. But this is exceptional because it's a Monday. If it was tomorrow it wouldn't be as much. Maybe I'll have one less staff in and do a section instead. If I come in and only do this, I'll just be wandering about.

CHAPTER ONE
PLACEMENT

THE RESTAURANT

The restaurant is Soho Soho, on the junction of Frith Street and Bateman Street, London W1. At the heart, as its name indicates, of Soho. Half a millennium ago the area was a royal hunting lodge – hence the name, from the hunting cry of Soho! – now it boasts as dense a population of eating places as anywhere in Britain, and possibly the world. On a fifty-yard stretch of Bateman Street to nearby Greek Street are, the restaurant aside, some nine establishments: the Dog and Duck and the Carlisle Arms pubs; a couple of sandwich bars – Richmond's and the Blue Room; and there are Chinese food at Wok Wok, Indian at the Golden Oven, modern British at Ego, and Italian at Lorelei and La Capannina. Stand on the corner of Frith Street, gaze south to Old Compton Street, Soho's 'High Street', and there are thirteen more. From individual pubs and branches of the ubiquitous chains, from sandwich bars and caffs to ethnic and gender-based (the area is also the country's gay capital), to media-haunted members' only clubs to top-of-the-line eateries, Soho offers literally thousands of places to eat and drink. Soho Soho, the flagship restaurant of the Groupe Chez Gérard, stands among the top 10 per cent, serving both Mediterranean-based 'fine dining' food in an upper restaurant (with an adjacent private room for parties of anything up to sixty people) and a faster, less formal and mainly grill-based version in a downstairs Rôtisserie, seating another 100.

THE KITCHEN

The kitchen is on the first floor. Approximately thirty feet by twenty, the size of a good-sized sitting room in a substantial London house. It has two entrances. One, through a swinging door, gives on to a narrow corridor, which runs left along the front of the kitchen, from which the food appears via a pair of serving hatches cut into the party wall to be taken into the dining room by attendant waiters, walking a few paces along past a small service bar – supplying drinks and coffee to the customers – through another pair of doors giving access to the restaurant. To its right the corridor runs maybe ten feet before turning left, passing a computer- and file-filled cubbyhole with a couple of chairs and over-crammed desks that serves as the kitchen's main office and past that through the door that leads into the private room or 'salon'. Diagonally across from the office, at the corridor's turn, is a table covered with a cloth, on which cleaned cutlery or plates are placed. The corridor itself contains a doorless 'cupboard', holding a couple more computers, an alcove with a Xerox machine and the metal sliding door of a service lift, which is used mainly for bringing up alcohol from the mesh-enclosed basement storage room. (The basement also holds the staff changing rooms, lockers and washroom, and stores cleaning chemicals, surplus glass- and tableware, extra chairs, a large chest freezer and a noticeboard devoted to announcements from the Group.) Along the corridor are a number of cupboards, at eye-level, holding dry goods (salt, pepper, olive oil, the olives and nuts that form part of every table setting), napkins, table linen, a variety of plates. There is room beneath them for a shelf on which loaves of bread are piled, ready to be sliced into baskets. Opposite these, on the outside of the kitchen wall, are a variety of notices, plus a set of hooks on to which waiters place the orders they have written on their pads at tableside. A large notice warns against leaning through the serving hatches when the heavy fire shutters – operated only in emergency – are descending. An internal staircase goes down to the Rôtisserie on the ground floor. The kitchen's second, rear exit opens on to the building's back stairway. Above are a number of offices – the usual Soho media mix; below it reaches a narrow alleyway, which ends in a door on to Bateman Street. This alley contains a number of wheelie bins – colour-coded black or yellow – taking refuse for daily processing by rubbish and 'pigswill' men, as well as a rubbish compactor. A circular metal staircase serves as a fire escape from the upper floors. The two Bateman Street sandwich bars, their frontages adjacent to this service entrance, also have back doors into the alley. At various times of the day you can find staff from any of the kitchens enjoying a smoke. The alley tends, inevitably, to some grubbiness; the stairs, up and down which pass the morning's deliveries and a continuous procession of chefs making their way between the two kitchens, can be slippery. Outside the kitchen door, despite a stern wall-mounted notice demanding the contrary, there is often food, either just delivered and ready for disposal around the kitchens' fridges and stores, or awaiting further cooking, typically the outsized stockpots filled with chicken carcasses, ready for the rest of the ingredients – calves' feet, vegetables, herbs, wine and water – that will reduce down through hours of slow simmering to make the daily portion of stock, the primary building block of so many dishes. As well as food, empty boxes rest here for a while before a kitchen porter removes them to the bins below. And if you go up rather than down the stairs, there's a roof, giving on to a variety of small offices, with a vista of similar Soho rooftops and a battery of air-conditioning vents, spewing the stench of a thousand menus into the air.

Inside, the kitchen's 600 square feet of floor are covered in white quarry tiles. Not that many of those feet are visible: this is no monster layout and the equipment, for storage, preparation and cooking, plus the inevitable boxes and sacks of incoming food, leave few tiles open for inspection. Professional kitchens are hot, crowded and noisy. This one is no exception. And in addition to the clustering inanimate objects are the human ones: the brigade of chefs. On a good day, i.e. one in which no one has called in sick, gone on holiday or simply left, there should be five chefs (the head chef and one each for the meat or 'sauce' section, the fish section, the larder section and the pâtisserie), plus two kitchen porters. All these thread their way constantly from worktop to fridge, from section to stove and thus along the narrow walkways that remain. The walls are also tiled, the usual ceramic, tinted reddish-brown, up to ceiling height. Some of the tiles are cracked and, if all are clean, none sparkle. This is not a new installation. The ceiling is painted cream – tired would be the kindest description: a working kitchen, with its steam, its grease, its spatters, its inevitable dirt, however regularly scoured, does not – and should not – contend for an *Interiors* magazine feature. Striplights shine down. The walls, where they are not obscured by equipment, supplies or plastic boxes of prepared foods, are regularly punctuated with notices: guides to preparing meat and fish; a colour chart of chopping boards headed 'Prevent Cross Contamination' (a red board for raw meat, blue for raw fish, yellow for cooked meats, green for salads and fruits, brown for vegetables, white for dairy products), hygiene rules, 'no smoking' and 'now wash your hands' signs, another advising 'don't risk it, wear it' ('it' being rubber gloves, goggles and aprons, although only the last seem general here; KPs, primarily washers-up, favour rubber gloves as well); there are staff work rotas, *mise en place* instructions (dish-specific preparation sheets), sheets detailing the parties that have been arranged for the salon, and the food they will be given. Above the hatches through which the finished, plated food is distributed to the waiters, is an electric fly-killer. There are two clocks.

If, like a chef arriving for work, you enter the kitchen through the back door, the layout, moving first around side and back walls, is as follows. To the immediate left of the door are small metal shelves, holding an odds-and-ends collection of kitchen bric-à-brac. Today there is also a Hobart mixer marked 'Broken – do not use'. Turn right and there is the kitchen's right-hand wall. It is dominated by two large walk-in fridges. The one on the right holds fish and meat; the other salad, fruit and vegetables. Plastic boxes of ingredients, all labelled as to content, date of production and the chef who did the work, plus *mise en place* (literally food that has been 'set in place', in other words prepared for later use), sit on the shelves. They are ordered with newest at the bottom, oldest at the top. That facilitates stock-taking and ensures that the supplies are used in chronological order. The fridges swing shut automatically, but an internal handle ensures that no one freezes to death. Between the walk-ins is another stand of metal shelving, holding a couple of spare kitchen-towel rolls, a gallon of olive oil, a can opener, a couple of screwdrivers, an industrial-sized roll of cling-film, more bric-à-brac, the odd box of fruit or vegetables. Beyond the walk-ins is a third fridge, a larger version of the domestic type, used to store *mise en place*. At the end of this right-hand wall is the platewash, a six-foot square set off but open to the main kitchen. This houses a large dish-washing machine, a comparably large sink, its mixer taps equipped with a high-pressure hose for the preliminary scouring of plates, and, on the kitchen's front wall, immediately next to the service door, a metal table on which incoming waiters dump used plates and cutlery. At the end of the table is a bin into which they scrape remains: today's gourmet food, tomorrow's pigswill. Opposite this table, next to the dishwasher, is a metal rack, where newly washed plates, cutlery, cups and saucers and cutting boards are piled.

Returning to the back door and turning left, the back wall of the kitchen has a six-foot metal work table at right angles to the wall. Here incoming food is prepared following the morning deliveries, before being placed in containers and then put into a fridge. Fish and meat will arrive cut 'according to spec', i.e. the specifications ordered from his suppliers by the head chef, but more preparation is needed before the food can be put away. Sides of fresh salmon will be cut into serving portions, kidneys stripped of their fat and freshly wrapped in caul fat, and duck legs placed in a dry marinade of garlic cloves and herbs, fillets of beef wrapped in clingfilm (which will hold them together when they are sliced later in the day.) Next to this prep table is a blast chiller, among the major kitchen innovations of modern times. This 'super-fridge' is not a deep freeze, but has the ability to reduce temperatures within seconds, ensuring hygiene, making cooking times more accurate (food taken off the heat still 'cooks' until it is properly cool; the chiller accelerates the process enormously), and hugely diminishing the need to reject food that has lost its initial freshness. Behind the prep table, at right angles to the chiller, is another large 'domestic' fridge. It opens on to the next section of the kitchen, the far corner of the back wall, which contains the pâtisserie. Set into the wall is a low-level store cup-board (wedged under the overhang formed by the external stairs) filled with flour, sugar, cooking chocolate and similar ingredients. The pâtisserie chef has his own prep table, with a (working) Hobart blender, an oven and, when the back wall turns right on to the kitchen's left-hand wall, a small wash-hand basin. A metal shelf runs at eye-level along the length of this wall. In the patisserie area it holds a microwave oven, a number of propane/butane blow torches (for, among other things, *crème brûlée*) and plastic containers of premade biscuits and sweets. As ever, all are comprehensively labelled. A file, secured to the wall, shows colour pictures of every dish prepared by the pastry chef, plus its ingredients and method of preparation.

The wall is also fronted by a number of waist-high fridges-cum-worktops. These stainless-steel fridges have either drawers or the 'normal' opening doors. This wall has two with drawers, four with doors.

The worktop contines the length of the wall and the bulk of it is used by the 'larder' chef, usually a junior or 'commis', preparing cold starters. On his portion of the shelf are plates, on which the starters will go, and more boxes. At the far end of the shelf, immediately next to the front wall, are a run of blue ring-binders containing the kitchen's immediate records (longer-term archiving is relegated to the office). In them reside variously food-delivery temperature charts (meat and fish must arrive off the van at a maximum of -5 degrees (they will be checked before the incoming invoice is signed); fridge temperature-control information (fridges are checked every day, first thing in the morning, late at night); sheets detailing the make-up of each receipe, whether current or no longer served; original copies of *mise en place* descriptions, food-order sheets, safety material covering the chemicals used in the kitchen (for washing up and cleaning floors). Finally, there is a wall-mounted phone.

The last, front wall of the kitchen, shared with the corridor that runs out to the restaurant itself and extending as far as the service door, is in essence more of the same. A further mixture of drawer and door fridges underneath another steel worktop provides the chefs with workspace and storage. A couple of plastic boxes, filled with warm water, are used for knives, keeping them clean between use. Hot knives also cut more efficiently. Again an eye-level shelf runs the length of the worktops; as well as the usual bits and pieces it has a small radio (with a fork, its tines jammed into a broken socket, as an aerial). A clip of *mise en place* sheets hangs from a hook (a list of days along the top, a list of dishes on the current menu — wrapped cod, cleaned scallops, hummus, chickpea salad, gremolata, risotto, and so on — down the side: each must be ticked *per diem*); a set of chef's knives, rolled up in their case, sits alongside them. There are a number of double plugs. A box holds a selection of squeezy bottles, not a lot different from the ones which contain tomato sauce or mustard in a junk-food caff. These are grander: they hold, respectively, tapenade oil, balsamic oil, aïoli, olive oil and lemon oil.

Two 'sections' work this front area: fish to the left, meat to the right. Between them is the pass, the final stop-off for every dish, where it is assembled or 'plated', checked (and sometimes replated) by the head chef or his stand-in and handed over to a waiter. Physically the pass is essentially an open hatch above the worktop. Metaphorically it is a culinary assembly line, where the whole process comes to a climax, the cooked food assembled as a dish. Watching this assemblage the viewer is struck by the quite literal 'hands-on' aspect of the process. The primary object – the piece of meat or fish – is probably placed on the plate with tongs or a palette knife, but vegetables and garnishes are usually positioned by hand. Like a model poised for her sashay along the catwalk, the dish is primped and teased into perfection. Then wrecked with the first descent of the punter's knife and fork.

Beneath the pass is a hot cupboard where dishes can, if necessary, be held in waiting. Underneath that section of the shelf which runs in front of it is a heat-lamp, keeping the dishes hot as they sit waiting for a waiter. The shelf also holds the main, hi-tech form of communication between the cooking staff and the front of house. The Remanco machine, a relatively new invention, allows waiters to key in their orders on a screen in the dining room, which in turn sends the information through to the kitchen, where order slips are printed out, ready for processing by the chefs. It is not an infallible method – even the best programmer fails in the face of a picky customer's specific demands, and waiters have to add the extra information by hand – but it has become a basic of the contemporary kitchen.

Thus the kitchen walls, with the attendant equipment pushing out into the available space. What remains is not, however, open. Immediately behind the pass is an island area, perhaps fifteen feet long and composed of two parts back to back, which holds the stoves and behind them the potwash. The latter is the province of a KP, whose continuous task it is to keep up with the flow of heavy pots and pans, saucepans and such items as the chinoise (a fine-mesh sieve) that are being used up during a service. The potwash comprises two large sinks and a couple of wash-hand basins (one at either end of the sinks). Rolls of paper kitchen towel are secured to the wall (another is available near the platewash). This KP is also responsible for operating the large potato masher, mounted on its movable tripod next to the sinks, and for such basic cooking jobs as washing vegetables and salad and cleaning mussels. Under the sinks sit the large pans used for roasting; other pans can be found stashed away beneath any available surface. Finally, the stoves, the powerhouse of any kitchen. Facing them, and running from left to right there is first a low-level gas burner (perhaps eighteen inches off the floor), which is reserved for the hundred-litre stockpots which simmer most of the day. (Until recently stockpots could be left on all night; new health and safety regulations have ended the practice.) Next to this is a deep-fryer usually used for chips, although oven chips are becoming increasingly popular, then three large stoves, two of them 'solid tops' (sheets of steel with burners hidden beneath them – heat varies as to the position of the pan: the edges are the coolest) and between them, the third one with four burners. All have large ovens. They are fed by gas, running through outsize pipes far larger than the narrow gauge of the domestic stove supply. These stoves, pouring out intense heat, have perhaps two feet between them and the pass and the sections which flank it. It is here, in this narrow corridor, that the main cooking is done. Above the stoves is a large canopy, taking away at least a proportion of the fumes and vapours that rise over the stoves and create a heat haze, wavy air currents reminiscent of a summer's day, as the saucepans and frying pans do their work. It is incessantly noisy, but it does not take long to blank out the sound, reducing it to no more than vaguely heard aural wallpaper.

(And the noise is worth it: the heat in a kitchen bereft of air-conditioning is appalling. How chefs managed when such equipment was as yet uninvented beggars the imagination. Not for nothing the endless consumption of cheap wine that permeates Orwell's tales of his work in a pre-war Paris hotel.) The canopy has beneath it a wide shelf, on which the potwash KP places the freshly cleaned saucepans and similar equipment, ensuring that no chef need ever lack these essential tools.

Downstairs the Rôtisserie kitchen is a cut-down version of the main cooking space. It has one four-burner stove, one hardtop, a deep-fryer and, given the style of menu, both an eye-level grill and a griddle. The potwash and platewash are combined. There are the usual fridges beneath worktops, a larder section with its fridge and worktop, several large, but not walk-in fridges and a couple of worktops. Upstairs the restaurant itself, a peaceful and almost spacious area after the claustrophobia of the kitchen, holds twenty-two tables capable of serving sixty-two 'covers', that is individual diners, in a long windowed room looking over Frith Street. The *salon privé*, for parties, can take up to sixty guests. A marble-floored Italianate, L-shaped room, its chairs are covered in alternate dark blue and maroon. The main, long table is usually laid – parties are frequent, and around Christmas provide an invaluable boost to the restaurant's income.

CHAPTER TWO
THE CHEF

The chef is Andrew Parkinson. Thirty-three, third among thirteen children (his prematurely widowed mother remarried and two broods were combined), he was born in the working-class town of Ellesmere Port on the Manchester Ship Canal in Merseyside. Surviving the 1980s, with its widespread downsizing, the port remains a major industrial centre: Burmah Oil, Castrol and Shell UK, as well as Vauxhall Motors, are all there; Andrew's stepfather works for Van Leer, makers of oil drums. The town thrives, with its pubs, social clubs and nightspots, but the gourmet cooking revolution, however popular it may have become in nearby Manchester, in further-off Leeds or in other once-derided cities outside the M25, is neither available nor especially desired. Yet people eat, they go out for meals, and others must cook them. One of them, at sixteen, was school-leaver Andrew Parkinson. But unlike the much-publicised young head chefs who have made their way via the kitchens of such culinary grandees as the Roux brothers, Pierre Koffman or Nico Ladenis, Andrew began his career in a much less glamorous world.

THE FLORIDA COCKTAIL YEARS

When I was at school I did cookery. Mum was a good family cook, but I didn't particularly have any home background in cooking. I just thought, 'I like cooking, I'll try that course.' It was home economics then: scones, flans, sponges, Scotch eggs, apple pies, shortbread fingers, gingerbread men. And you had to do knitting. But I loved it. I used to make all the Swiss rolls, the sponges, for my mum's friends in the street. Of course at school cookery was for girls, not boys, and we were known as pansies. But I'd volunteered for it. I got sent to Ince-B, the power station, on a two-week training course. I was in the works canteen, where they made big quiches, spaghetti bologneses, fish and chips. Working seven till three. Getting up in the morning at five-thirty, getting on to a minibus with thirteen ladies – because that's what most chefs were as far as I was concerned, ladies in canteens who cooked the food – and when I got to work I peeled onions for two weeks and just cried my eyes out, peeling onions. When I left they said to me, 'You can always apply for a job if you fancy it, because you'd make a good chef.' Only two people in that class are chefs now, myself and a friend. Later on, when I was working at Quaglino's, he was a sous chef at the Ritz, next door. We'd both gone from a small classroom making fairy cakes and Scotch eggs to working in two of London's biggest hotels and restaurants. At the time I wouldn't have believed it: all they told me was I was going to be working in Greasy Joe's Café.

I left school in 1983 and I decided to try and be a chef full-time. I joined a two-year YTS catering course: the HCITB, Hotel Catering Industries Training Board. The first year we did a lot of work together in a group. Some of the girls were going to be receptionists, some of the boys hotel managers, some waitresses, some chefs. We worked in the Port, staying together as a group in a small hotel, twenty of us in their conference room listening to lectures. At the start it was all theory: learning about waiting on, being a chef, what a KP's job was like.

Then we got sent out to placements. I spent the first three

months in the Witch's Kitchen in Chester. It had been going for years. When people were out shopping they wanted a nice place to have a quick meal, not costing too much. And that's what the Witch's Kitchen provided. Pseudo-Tudor outside, awesome carpets inside. No matter — it was very popular. It was called a restaurant, but really this was upper-class café cooking. Deep-fried everything — which was what the public expected anyway — and everything came with chips: chicken, egg, sausage, deep-fried chicken in a basket, lasagne, chilli con carne, chicken curry, mixed grills — all with chips. I was a waiter, didn't get a job in the kitchen at all. I was waiting to get into the kitchen, to start cooking, but when I saw that kitchen I never thought I'd ever want to be a chef. The owner just grabbed people off YTS so they'd work for free, tried to save as much money as possible. Buckets of potatoes sitting outside the back door, in the street; packet soup made up, poured into buckets and sitting outside in a 200-space car park. But they got away with it. They were cooks, though, not chefs.

Still, when after four weeks they offered me a full-time job, I accepted it gratefully. Except they put me behind the bar. I wanted to be a chef and I was working behind a bar. But I was only sixteen, not legally allowed to drink, and it was quite funny, they were sending me down the off licence to buy vodka and they'd serve me, no problem. But the manager never allowed me in the kitchen. That was the way it was: the chefs in the hotels and restaurants in the area had been there for years and wouldn't give up their jobs. They ran the place and people worked for them, ran round for them; no way would they give up their position.

When I'd got just three months left on my HCITB course they moved me again, to a place called the Woodhey Hotel in

Little Sutton. And once my three months were up they took me on full-time and that was my first chef's job. I thought it was great. I loved it there, worked there for a couple of years and had a great time. I was a chef. I was getting £53 before tax, probably £40 in hand – £10 for Mum, £10 for my motorbike, £20 to live on for the week. But then, just going from the YTS, which had been £25 a week, to £53 a week was all right. Doubled my earnings. I didn't really pay much tax because I hadn't earned any money. When I got a wage rise, then the tax started. That was £64 a week. All the shifts then were doubles: nine a.m. to three-fifteen, then five or six p.m. start again ready for seven p.m. opening, and the restaurant closed at ten, with you home at ten-thirty. Of course when you're doing that five days a week, your social life goes down the pan.

The food, like most hotel food at that level, was more *Daily Star* than Michelin star: prawn cocktails, Florida cocktails, melon boats and pâté. All the beef was roasted. Not beef with sauce or anything, just grilled this, roasted that. There was always beef on the menu, always turkey à la king or chicken à la king, chicken curry. No vegetarian dishes in those days. The fish would be rolled-up plaice. I was a commis chef, the lowest of the low. The chef made all the main things, all the soups and sauces, and I just had to open the tins of Maggi or Knorr; even the asparagus in the chicken and asparagus was tinned. All the desserts were bought in ready-made – strawberry gâteaux, Cointreau ice-creams, mints in packets, cheesecakes. All just put on a sweet trolley. All the sauces came out of tins. Cheeses were just Cheddar and Stilton – Stilton was quite glamorous. I also worked on the starter section: prawn cocktails and Florida cocktails, half a silver goblet filled with lettuce, prawns and Marie-Rose sauce with a lemon wedge and the other full of these disgusting tinned grapefruit segments and fresh orange segments (the only thing that was fresh). And topped off with a tinned bright red cherry. Basically that describes my early repertoire of top-class nosh . . . not sea bass, caviare or lobsters . . . tinned grapefruit and cherries! This wasn't unusual: the Woodhey Hotel exemplified the culinary standard of all hotel food at that level. As far as I knew, this was the only way to do the job.

The Woodhey was renowned for its dinner parties, which were mostly on Fridays and Saturdays. Even more around Christmas: from the last week in November till Christmas there was a dinner-dance every night – tables of twenty, tables of fourteen, office staff, big works outings, a cabaret, the whole bit. About 350 punters would turn up each night throughout Christmas and tuck into something like rollmops, pâté with toast, melon boats, Florida cocktail. Followed by roast beef. Then apple pie and ice-cream. Same things every time. Ten quid a head inclusive. You'd have checks coming in for 4 prawn cocktails, 5 orange juice, 3 pâtés, 8 beef, 2 pork and that was it. The chefs would get four sirloins, cut 'em up, cook them in the afternoon, and slice it all up and put it in hot plates with the sauce over them, and just warm it through when they needed them; occasionally there'd be something else: dry chicken or turkey à la king and 'fish surprise' (in other words Mersey trout). I can't remember them having vegetarian dishes at that time. It was fish, meat and vegetables. Nothing else. The vegetables would go in the bain-marie at seven and people came in at nine and there were the roast potatoes and beans. The veg chef just had to blanch the vegetables again, put 'em in a bowl, put some butter and parsley over the top and that was it. Terrible. When they ran out of the first lot the chef would get frozen beans out of packets, cook up some more, and put them into the bain-marie with a bit of butter, bit of salt. He kept filling it up as the night went on. Trays of beef in the oven, taken out, slotted into a bain-marie, pour stock over the top, and keep it hot and coming.

Of course you don't always get high standards in good restaurants in London. I've watched French graduates of three-star kitchens using their full body weight to squeeze the blood out of *filet mignons* and turning a medium steak to a well-done one in seconds. I've watched in horror as chefs have hurled beautiful *châteaubriands* into the deep-fat fryer, microwaved veal chops, made thin sauce from brackish greasy water in the steam table. This basically means you've got a bain-marie in front of you and you've made a sauce which is getting too thick because the bain-marie's sort of boiling and not just ticking away. You put a bit of water in the sauce to thin it down, but then the bain-marie's got grease in it from things that have spilt over and everything. Disgusting. I've seen a tomato sauce, made from a tin in an Italian restaurant, sit there for twenty-four hours and then get used the next day — in the six hours they were closed the rats were probably looking into it. That's London, which is supposed to be smart, but when people do that kind of thing, there's no difference from what can go on in the provinces.

Then somebody offered me a job in a brand-new hotel, the Regency Hotel, in Ellesmere Port. The chef had previously worked at the Woodhey, but he'd left before I arrived. He had his bar at the front — the Victoria Bar — hotel rooms, a small restaurant and a large banqueting room. The intention was to have discos in there on the weekends. They paid me an extra £10 a week. Two characters owned the hotel. One of them, his dad had brought him up from antique dealing, and they'd turned themselves into millionaires. The other bloke was a hairdresser.

They wanted this place to be known. They built a kitchen on the back of this huge dining area, which was to be used as a dinner-dance/cabaret room adjoining an old hall, which they turned into a hotel with about thirty rooms and a small *à la carte* kitchen and restaurant. The cabaret evenings were busy, it was mental! Or, as I should say, diabolical. Most of the staff were agency workers from outer space, the chefs didn't really gel, too many clashing attitudes, and too many girls washing up pots who thought they should have been walking up catwalks. But the food wasn't the important thing: people packed the place out because the cabaret acts were all top class: anyway, no one can tell me they came for the egg mayonnaise or Florida cocktails!

At the time Ellesmere Port was going through changes. So the owners decided to make some changes of their own. Out went the Friday night dinner-dance of old, in came their own style of dinner-dance and also a new head chef. The main room was fitted out with a £100,000 lighting system, which created this fantastic light show. The idea was to sell tickets at £5 each: that paid for your entrance fee and a meal, which was a plate of chilli con carne and rice. The only reason for the meal was that it justified the supper licence. People had to be there to eat. So from Friday night we just made pots and pots of chilli. So now it wasn't a dinner-dance, it was a disco.

As far as the food went it was the same old thing — we got it all ready and chucked it all out. These chefs would have trained in the army perhaps, or in big railway hotels — lots of chefs, lots of food, plenty of covers — and they could run a restaurant, no doubt about it. But fine dining didn't come into it. You spent all day making prawn cocktails, coarse chicken liver pâté served with a Cumberland sauce — a sweet jam and port reduction, an easy thing to make. So despite all their plans, things started to go really really wrong. The team wasn't helped by one guy who was the biggest idiot I've ever met. He spent all day on this food, trying to tell you what it was all about. But it wouldn't have got past my Rôtisserie kitchen downstairs today, or any run-of-the-mill London rôtisserie: it was that bad. There was another chef who had always been more interested in skirts than food and this time he'd left his wife, moved out of the house to be with some waitress. His replacement was better and he brought in a good sous chef, but the food didn't really change much. The organisation was much better. The chef (he was six foot six, really frightened people and got them all in line) put his foot down. Before that the staff had been getting away with murder. But the food was still what you'd expect in a provincial place: chicken chasseur in the *à la carte* restaurant, steak bordelaise, chicken Kiev, *entrecôte* with three different sauces and baked trout with almonds. In the cabaret room it was bar food, such as curry, gammon, lasagne and cold meat salads. The fish dishes were like glazed plaice and sole – never any tuna, or salmon, or sea bass. Again, that's what the people wanted. You might have learnt the basics at college – making stocks and sauces and so on – but when you walked into a hotel it was in tins, all tins. And the desserts were bought in here too – a bloke would come down from Liverpool: 'What d'you want this week, mate?' And you'd take what you wanted from the back of the van – that was your desserts. We had a carvery in the bar at lunchtime – sweet and sour pork, curries. All the roast potatoes were chucked in the deep-fat fryer, then put in the oven and that was it.

I worked at the hotel for about three years and had a great time. I was a commis. I thought I was being a good chef. When I look back, I'm shocked. But at that time, the Regency was one of the best places to eat in Ellesmere Port, and what I considered good then, I'd consider garbage now. Of course I realise now that all I learnt there was how to work in kitchens, nothing about food. Just how to do my job. What you learned was organisation: the challenge was to get ready in time, keep everything clean, do your hours. But actual cooking; nothing. I didn't think about it then, I was just working to have money to spend outside. Just a job. The truth was that I never really took it seriously enough, I only went to work to pay for my motorbike and for my snooker, which I played literally every day. On Saturday I'd work in the morning, get a lift to Anfield to watch Liverpool and come straight back to work after the game. It was football, in fact, that would make the big change in my career. It was April 1987, Liverpool had just lost to Arsenal in the League Cup Final, I went to the pub to drown my sorrows and after that, pretty drunk, I went back into work to cook for a full house of guests – we were doing a Bob Champion dinner, a charity event. Going from one kitchen to another I tried to jump off some steps and I fell over. The chef saw me, realised I was drunk and told me, 'If you do one thing wrong tonight, you're out.' I thought, 'Bollocks,' and gave in my notice. I didn't realise it then, but that was the smartest thing that I'd done in years and it certainly changed my career for the good.

Then, as now, the cooking in the majority of provincial hotels and restaurants remains a world distant from the advances in London and in the landmark establishments dotted around the country. The foundation, sadly inescapable, of every negative stereotype suffered by British cooking. As Andrew discovered, what passed as a 'chef' in Ellesmere Port, barely qualified him for a job in a 'proper' kitchen. In the event he found one, at the five-star Gleneagles Hotel in Scotland, removed as far as possible, both geographically and, more importantly, culinarily, from Merseyside. A year there, in which he went from a terrified novice to winning a much-coveted Employee of the Month award, turned him from a glorified tin opener into a professional chef. From Gleaneagles he moved in 1988 to Billesley Manor, a large country hotel near Stratford-upon-Avon, which cooked modern British cuisine. As first commis, part of a brigade of seven chefs cooking for a seventy-cover restaurant, he was initially responsible for the complete running of the larder section (i.e. cold starters), moving up to the sauce section (meat and fish dishes – hot starters – sauces and stocks). He was made Employee of the Year in 1989. In 1990 he moved to his first London kitchen, in the 418-bedroom Royal Lancaster Hotel on Bayswater Road, working in the seventy-cover fine dining restaurant serving English and French cuisine. Commencing as a demi chef de partie on the sauce section, he progressed upwards from there to senior chef de partie, responsible for the ordering and running of the kitchen. After the Royal Lancaster he moved again, in 1992, to Odette's, one of north London's most popular restaurants. As sous chef he was second-in-command, and regularly stood in for head chef Paul Holmes. In 1995 he joined Quaglino's, formerly a fashionable nightclub, now revamped as a restaurant by the Conran Group. As junior sous and latterly sous chef he managed an eighty-strong brigade of chefs, preparing food for a 338-cover restaurant. Leaving Quaglino's in late 1997 he spent six months in a variety of less than satisfactory jobs before being asked to open a brand-new restaurant: the Soho Brewing Company in Covent Garden. This done he moved in late 1998 to Soho Soho, the flagship restaurant of the Groupe Chez Gérard. The fruits of his work in all these kitchens, and the experiences gained therein, underpin the book that follows.

CHAPTER THREE

THE KITCHEN HIERARCHY

The cooking staff in a professional kitchen, from the head chef downwards, are known as the brigade. The word, with its image of military hierarchy, was imported, like many kitchen terms, from France. Its origins lie in the Italian *brigata*, a company, crew or 'rout of good fellows' and beyond that, with a satisfactory irony for anyone who has been a member of such a 'rout', from the verb *brigare*, to brawl, wrangle or fight. From the bottom up the ranks run thus: commis, first (and sometimes second) commis, demi chef de partie, chef de partie, senior chef de partie, the relatively rare chef tournant (the kitchen's jack of all trades, an all-purpose 'stand-in' substituting for absent or holidaying chefs, and capable of working on any section, preparing everything from starters to sauce), junior sous chef, sous chef, senior sous chef, head chef and executive head chef. The size of brigade varies with the size of kitchen and not every rank is invariably found or required. A small kitchen is unlikely to run to a first commis, a junior sous or an executive head chef; a large kitchen or a major hotel, where more than one kitchen is running under the same head chef, will have these and more, with individual senior sous chefs running mini-brigades of their own, thus giving the establishment several first commis, several junior sous and so on. A small restaurant might get by with a head chef, a sous, a chef de partie and a single commis. Food quality, of course, has no bearing on numbers.

Given the demands of the work – long days on your fee with barely a chance for a proper rest, not to mention the continuous mental pressure of cooking for a busy restaurant – cooking is by no means a well-paid job. The superstars can, and do, make serious money; the majority of chefs, especially those yet to become masters of their own kitchen, do not. As far as pay goes, the average wage for a sous chef would be between £20,000 and £28,000 a year; junior sous chef between £18,000 and £22,000 a year; chef de partie, senior chef de partie, £15,000 to £18,000 a year; demi chef de partie, £11,000 to £15,000 a year; commis chefs, £9,000 to £11,000 a year. A head chef can get from £30,000 upwards, some of it a production bonus; the head chef in a big restaurant can be looking at £70,000 and more.

The following, starting from the bottom, are the main ranks of chef.

THE COMMIS CHEF

The commis, from the French *commis*, a deputy or clerk, therefore one who is specially employed or commissioned, stands at the very bottom of the hierarchy, learning his or her trade and effectively a paid (albeit minimally paid) apprentice. As such the commis's primary duties are to help, to watch and to learn. Depending on the size of the kitchen a commis might be running their own section, usually the larder (for cold starters – the least demanding of dishes) or alternatively, in a large hotel for instance, there might be eight chefs on the larder section alone, and the commis would be the most junior of the eight. But if commis seems at times no more than a synonym for overworked, exploited dogsbody, then these early years are vital. This, says Andrew, is when you really do have to look, listen and learn; this stage can make or break your cheffing career.

I started off as a commis chef at the Gleneagles Hotel near Auchterarder in Scotland, running the starters section in the only five-star hotel outside London at the time. The larder at Gleneagles is a proper larder, where they do all the meat and fish prep. There were three set menus, different choices, and they rotated over an eight-day period. My responsibility was getting everything plated up in advance on the plate racks ready for serving. You'd expect to sell eighty prawn and watercress plates, thirty spinach and wild mushroom plates, seventy melon platters (three varieties of melon with a poppy-seed yoghurt) on a given night. So with the prawn dish what you'd do is plate up everything in advance. Which meant starting off by laying out all eighty plates around you. Then you went back to the first and ladled out a dribble of sauce, all round the eighty plates; then back to the first plate, pick it up, turn it round so the sauce covered the whole base, run down to the last plate; then back to the beginning to put the prawns on, all the way there, all the way back. You had to be speedy. The kitchen operated twenty-four hours a day. For example the breakfast chef – big Jerry, at least twenty-four stone – started at one or two a.m. You had a room-service breakfast chef and Jerry, the main restaurant breakfast chef. There was one big room for breakfast-room cold service, buffet-style for starters, then the hot food came out plated from the kitchen. The bakers would start at midnight – all the bread was baked there. There was a night chef who did room service. When the night shift went, another room-service chef came on. This would be just one person. But somebody joined the breakfast chef at six a.m. The day chefs started at about eight a.m. The main thing you did was get out your equipment before anybody else. That was drilled into me. Where's this? Where's that? Why didn't you get it first thing this morning? Get that now – you don't have it? Nick it off him. Everyone protected their equipment and their *mise en place* with their life, and an attitude. Even if you ran out in the middle of service, you needed more parsley or something, it was, 'Fuck off, get your own, don't come near mine.' Rotten attitudes. Every morning the sous chefs had a meeting about how many covers they were expecting to be doing, any parties, any outside catering, that kind of thing, and if you weren't in that meeting they'd send someone for you. They wouldn't knock and say, 'You're late.' Your door would get kicked in. There was an Irish chef de partie, Alan: at one of these meetings he leant against the wall and they were telling him, 'This is what's going on today' . . . and he slid down the wall and hit the floor and dropped his file. He just lost it, just went.

On a Sunday night, we'd do 440 covers in the restaurant; 140 of those would be *a la carte*, and what that meant was one chef, the one responsible, would just work his nuts off, working flat out to be ready for seven p.m. when the restaurant opened. And when the order checks started flying in, he was working even harder. I did the *hors d'oeuvres*, the set menus. So I always had three sets of starters on, but with different salads or whatever. I knew if I was prepped up, had thirty plates ready with baby spinach put on the plate, then I had to cook my mushrooms and orange sauce at the same time and plate it. On Saturday nights for Sundays, I had to make sure that in the fridge I had five trays of foie gras set in a jelly ready for the next day, so I could come in, cut it, plate it, wrap it on a trolley and have it ready. It was up to me to keep up with the advance prep. If I didn't, it meant big trouble.

Being a commis is quite hard, not just because of the work itself but because they're expecting you to know it all when you don't. You learn by writing things down and taking it all in. If you don't remember something, you have to ask again and again, and you don't want to do that because of the grief you get. So you need to take in as much as possible. At Gleneagles I went through all that, and thought, 'No, I ain't gonna take this shit,' and the only way to get over that was to learn, to prove to them I could do the job. So at the end of the day you write down the things you've done that day in your book. That's what I tell commis to do now: write it down and learn it. I used to sit down at night and draw a picture of how I set my bench up. And by doing that, you remember how you did it.

When someone coming into the business gets their first job, they'll be a commis, then a first commis for a couple of years. If they stay in the same place for longer, they'll stay as first commis for about two or three years. A first commis is basically just a glorified commis who's trying to move up in the world. Some places want to keep you as low as possible for as long as possible. From first commis they go to demi chef de partie. In a hotel you've got a lot of levels, so if you're a commis on a section you're doing everything for the chefs de partie on that section. The chefs de partie at a place like Gleneagles were responsible for running a section, with demi chefs de partie and commis chefs working for them. So a commis in that sort of kitchen would be there to do all the shitty jobs. But he'd be learning at the same time.

Once you get promoted to second or first commis you get more responsibilities. At Gleneagles you'd then be left in charge of sections now and again, when the chef de partie was off. On every section there'd be a chef de partie in charge of his little brigade. If it was a fish section, you'd have two chefs de partie, two demis, two first commis and a commis. Each service would have a chef de partie, a demi and a commis. But whatever you're actually doing, the big thing at that stage is that it's all about proving yourself and showing your own willingness to work and to learn.

THE CHEF DE PARTIE

Chef de partie, literally 'head of a team', is the next full rank up, and his junior, the demi or 'half' chef de partie, bridges the gap from the commis.

As a demi you've moved up a step, but you're still learning: how to run the section, how to explain to the commis how things should be done. I did my demi work at the Royal Lancaster in London, then got promoted to chef de partie. 'De partie' means you're in charge of a group of people. So to be a chef de partie you have to be seen to be capable of organising them. In a small restaurant it might only be a commis or two, but as a senior chef de partie, in big hotels usually, you're overseeing several people. At Soho Soho we've got two chefs per section, one for lunch, one for dinner. Being chef de partie in a full brigade involves running a section, and he'll have demi chefs and commis working for him. He'll run a section, and on his day off he'll leave it all set up for the demi chef de partie. It's the first time you get any managerial experience really, learn how to organise your week. You don't cook less, you just take more work on board. And still you're learning.

In my experience the nature of the job's changed a lot. When I was a first commis at Billesley Manor, the job I did would be a chef de partie's job now. I was doing twice as much as some of my chefs de partie do now. I was in charge of the stocks and sauces, the staff food, all the meat prep, all the garnishes, and then the service – the fish, the meat, any hot starters. I was doing seventy covers a night. You couldn't get a first commis to do that any more – he'd expect to be a chef de partie anyway. You've got a lot of so-called chefs de partie in London now, who couldn't do the job I was doing as first commis. I worked doubles, ten shifts a week. I was there lunch and dinner for five days a week. My chefs do six shifts each, and it's either lunch or dinner. Or they do one double. Ten years ago there was a lot of five doubles a week. You'd go in at nine a.m., out by three; back at six and out by ten p.m. Not long hours, but a very long day.

THE SOUS CHEF

The sous chef, from French 'sous', sub, is the head chef's immediate number two. In a large kitchen you find both junior sous and senior sous; in a smaller kitchen just the sous, who both assists the head chef and doubles for him when he is off. In military terms, if the commis is the poor bloody infantry, then the sous chef is the sergeant.

In a big kitchen the sous chef, especially the senior sous, doesn't do that much cooking. What the job's about at this level is being able to manage the kitchen and above all the people in it. This is where office work, paperwork, comes in. You've got rotas to do, things like that. At one stage at Quag's we had a full team of fifty-seven or fifty-eight chefs. There was a head chef, a senior sous, four sous, two junior sous. Out of the remainder, only ten were serious cooks. So forty of them are just there to do the job, not career-minded. In our place we have eighteen to nineteen chefs who hold the fort. They have to, because we're smaller. At Quag's I had to do rotas for fifty chefs – a nightmare. Seven shifts per person, 350 shifts to organise in a week.

I came from Odette's, which is a small restaurant with a small brigade, and I was cooking every shift, and suddenly I'm at Quaglino's and I'm not involved in the cooking any more, or not much, and I'm dealing with the administration. A sous chef is basically a kitchen manager. Our job was to make sure the kitchen ran for eighteen hours a day. Some people won't make it because they can't write a rota out for fifteen people. It is difficult, or it can be, but you should be able to do it at that level. Putting the right people in the right section at the right time. The sous chefs have to do the food ordering, order people around, train people. There are a lot of good cooks who can't manage people and to be a good sous chef you have to be able to do that too. Your only way out if you can't handle that is to get a job as head chef in a small restaurant, where you've got a sous chef to do it for you. Then your job would be to do the ordering, sign the invoices, make sure the staff get their days off and write the menus. No people management required.

A sous chef in a big place has to learn management. He's part of the management team and he's responsible to the people above him. So if he doesn't sort things out, the head chef will sort him out. And that's the way it's got to be done. And that's also what you've go to get across to the others: 'OK, we'll have a pint together after work, but when we're inside the kitchen if I don't get you to sort this out, I'll get grief off the old man.' It is like becoming a sergeant: you can't hang around with your old mates any more. When I was at Quag's I was managing fifty-eight people. In one way it's better than cooking: you get tossed in at the deep end as you do when you're a commis, but since it's management stuff you do get shown how to do things, although pretty soon it's a matter of your own confidence. You get to run the kitchen on a certain day and you need to know who you should be looking out for, what should be done at certain times, what should be cleared, where things should be, how they should work. It's best to watch the people above you and take note of what they're doing. But you can only be told so much. The rest is down to you and your personality – how you personally treat people, approach them. You just have to keep on eye on what the chef does, and on anyone else above you, and you're fine.

The senior sous is a total administrator. The chef's right-hand man. He's authority and he has to get things right: if the sous chefs have done something wrong, the head chef goes to the senior sous and tells him about it. Of course, that also means that when things are going wrong it's the senior sous who gets all the real shit from the head chef. On days like that it's not a job you want. A junior sous is part-chef, part-manager – he still does a bit of cooking: he can work on the sections half the week, and the other half of the week he's on the pass, doing the checks, managing the kitchen. So that's half cooking, half managerial. That's in a big place. In a small place you wouldn't have a junior sous. It would be sous chef, head chef, and that's it. At the moment I have a junior sous chef because it gives cover for when I'm on holiday and the sous chef has his nights off. Then the junior sous chef takes over. If you've got a senior chef de partie who's good at his job, but not quite what you want for a junior sous, you'll go and look elsewhere. But if he's good enough to promote, then that's what you do – and everyone else moves up a rank. If you're looking at it purely on administrative grounds, it's always to your advantage to promote in-house. If you can do it in-house, by say giving a chef de partie a couple of thousand more, you can save yourself £15,000 in extra costs. And you're not having to acclimatise someone new to the ways of the kitchen.

But being a manager cuts both ways. For me the problem with being a sous chef was that I didn't get to cook. I complained to myself when I left Quag's that I hadn't cooked for two years. But if you haven't been there, you don't understand. People would say, 'You've been a sous chef at Quag's for two years. Why can't you do this and that dish?' The commis, junior sous and chefs de partie were there to cook, the senior chef de partie was there to look after the other chefs de partie. But, as I say, the sous chef is there as a manager and some of them see it as an escape from doing the cooking. Anyway, whether you like it or not, it would have been impossible at Quag's for the sous chefs to cook on the sections when they're there to run a kitchen, as kitchen managers.

I love doing the cooking. And in a small kitchen, like Soho Soho, I can still do it. I'm not a remote head chef sitting in an office, checking out reports from my senior sous. The other night we were one down and I cooked. I love it, and anyway I need to keep in touch with what's going on. Though you can see it as a good thing and a bad thing – I wasn't actually doing the pass or the cooking because I really wasn't needed, but I felt like a spare, walking round prepping, doing other things. I have two boys running the front of the kitchen for me who are good enough to do it on their own. You think to yourself, 'Do they think I'm lazy?' Then you think, 'They're doing so well I'm not needed.' But if one of them goes off sick, you just get in there. I can go on every section and do it. Whereas at Quaglino's, someone else was running it; I was a sous chef and cooking was something other people did, and if I got called on to the sauce section in the middle of a busy service, I didn't know what was going on. You've got 140 covers waiting ready to be sent out because someone's got so much in the shit – that's why you've been called there – and they expect you to go on and say, 'Right, clear the way, both sides, I'll just walk through and everything will be all right.' But what actually happens is I'm thinking, 'What the hell's going on here? Help!' Your heart's going bang-bang. Everyone's watching: wow, the sous chef's been dragged on to the sauce, they'll be all right now. But you've got to get on there, hold your nerve and say, 'OK, this is what we'll do.' You bang it all up and all of a sudden it's all clear. You're all fine. They'll only panic if you panic. You get it sorted out, it goes and that's it. But you never really did any cooking. You'd cover a section, help on a section whenever you were required to. Otherwise, you were a kitchen manager, just like the sous chefs at Gleneagles were. But not everyone's like me: some sous chefs only want to manage, they don't want to cook any more. They can write the menus, oversee the staff, and stay out of the kitchens for ever. The downside is that this often turns them into loud-mouthed know-alls who will probably go a long way with their mouth rather than their hands.

Being a non-cooking sous chef does have its advantages, though. When I got the job at Soho Soho I was told by the interviewers they knew I was right for the job when I said I was in and out of the fridges every day at Quag's – the sous chefs and I cleaned them out every day, made sure they were spot on before we were even in the kitchen. And this woman knew she was going to employ me because I said that – it wasn't just about what I could do in a kitchen, it was about running one well, apart from just cooking the food.

THE HEAD CHEF

The head chef is the kitchen's supreme authority. His only superior is an executive head chef, a figure usually found in a large establishment, typically a Conran 'gastrodome' like Mezzo, where the executive head chef is responsible for two restaurants, which share between them a brigade of 120 chefs, or at a large hotel such as Gleneagles, where in Andrew's day there were three restaurants, plus regular hotel catering, all serviced by a 78-strong brigade of chefs. But elsewhere it is the head chef who is in charge. He may not own the restaurant, although such stars as Gordon Ramsay or Marco Pierre White do, but the kitchen is his domain. At the same time it is his responsibility. When all goes well, his name garners the applause (for all that the brigade may be cooking 'his' food), but when customers are deserting, when profits are down, when the kitchen is failing, it is he whose head is on the directors' chopping block.

As a head chef I've got to write menus, write the recipes to go with the menus, search for the best suppliers to supply me with exactly what I want for the menus — and arrange that the food supplied conforms to a specific size, weight, cut or whatever. I handle recruitment — that's hiring and firing; discipline; rotas; holiday planning for the whole of the kitchen brigade; giving out specific jobs to specific people; deciding when to promote people; running the kitchen; cooking in the kitchen; fridge management — keeping them as clean as possible all the time; management of the kitchen, which involves making sure the equipment is working all the time, is clean all the time; keeping the kitchen up to scratch for health and hygiene inspections; dealing with management issues, customer issues, staff issues. It just goes on and on, it's not just working in a kitchen, cooking.

First of all you've got to be able to cook. So you have to write a menu, you've got to research suppliers. You need recipes written out, menus written, sheets for people in the kitchen, you need to write out descriptions of the food – prep sheets – you need to work out daily prep sheets, so you need to work out when you write a menu exactly what's going to be in every fridge . . . Then there are management meetings to go to, profit and loss meetings – they're every two to three months. Now there's advert-ising promotions to organise. The auditor comes in once in, say, six months on the off-chance. You've got to do weekly stock-takes on Monday morning, and that's everything in the building. First day of the week starts at Monday lunch, so you stock-take on Monday morning. I can have everything sorted out by twelve-thirty. So we take a stock count of all the meats, the fish, fruit and veg, dairy products, ice-creams, etc, all the dry goods. Write down exactly what we've got in.

All the time you're making your way up through the kitchen you have to think, 'I want to be the best, I want everything I do to be as good if not better than someone above me.' That was my ambition when I was still a commis at Gleneagles, to be as good as my chef de partie – he was so fast. Then in the next job I looked out for the person above me, thinking, 'I'll try and do better than him.' You give him respect, you know he's good, but you want to do better. When I got to Quag's there were decent people above me and I had to aim to do better than them. But once you become head chef, that all stops. You have to do it yourself then. No one to look up to. Now you have to look down at those beneath you, and gain their respect. You've got to motivate people. You can either tell them nicely how to do it and perhaps they'll do it, or you just shout. You can tell someone nicely to do something, and they go, 'Oh yeah yeah,' and they won't do it. But if you shout, they won't forget and they will do it. Putting a little bit of fear about never goes amiss.

As head chef I have to think about the punters because they're the ones who eat the food and pay the wages, but before them it's the kitchen staff. I have to show them I've got the knowledge to do something they've not seen before, or, if they have, that I can cook it just as well. That's first and foremost. You could call it education. A few months ago we had stuffed sea bass *en paupiette* on the menu. For most of the staff the way I prepared it was something they'd never seen. So I explained it all to them. At the same time I was trying to educate the punters, showing them that you could have something more than just another fillet when it came to fish. I served it for two people as a whole fish at the table, so when they received it they would think, 'We've got two plates empty in front of us, we've got new potatoes, we've got lemon, we've got this fish, we've got sauce on the table – let's help ourselves.' For me, it's good for people to see the whole fish, stuffed, and do it themselves. And it's good for the staff to see something new.

Of course, if I have a day off and I'm at home, I have to know that my staff are thinking exactly like me, and you can't always guarantee that. They just want to get the food up, do the service, get cleaned down and go home. They've prepped all morning, got everything right, cooked it, the sauce is good, they've got it all sorted out, then we get service on, they start getting a bit frustrated because they're busy, get a bit angry, and then when it comes to putting the food on the plate at the last minute, they just want to knock it out because more checks are coming in from the waiters. That's the time where they might just think of chucking it out instead of getting it right.

Whatever happens in the kitchen I've got to deal with it and no two nights are ever the same. One evening I might get really annoyed with the restaurant staff, the front of house: they're being absolutely useless. They're just not as good as they're supposed to be. The head chef would like to have a lot of control over that, but you have to make sure you don't step over the line. If someone thinks you're rude, they could report you to management and you don't want that. After a night like that I'll go and speak to the restaurant manager, talk the problems through before the service and, hopefully, it'll be a calm night. An absolute dream. Another night, we might be one chef down and have forty people in the private dining room and a hundred in the restaurant. Understaffed and overbooked. So I need to make sure the kitchen runs as a kitchen. If we have an angry night, we have an angry night. You have to work out how to talk to people. If you're in the middle of a row and you can point out what they're doing wrong, fine. But if you're giving them grief for no reason, they'll react. They'll walk out, then I'll be down on staff in the kitchen and hated by the front of house. You have to treat people with some respect. It's only sensible. Working at Quaglino's or Gleneagles was a completely different thing, though. The head chef was god and he could do and say what he liked. Take Gleneagles. The head chef had a commis chef washing pots on Christmas night because he was in a bad mood with him. The chef doesn't think twice about it. If that commis chef leaves, he'll get someone else. If I did that here, my commis chef would leave. But I *wouldn't* do it.

THE CAREER

For all the dramas, the tensions, the pressure and the current media interest, working in a restaurant kitchen is a career much like any other. And if a good many are called, relatively few make the grade. It's tough and wearing and in the end, once again like any other career, the individual has to choose whether to stick it out. In many ways — although equipment is technically superior, and the English, surprising perhaps even themselves, have finally rebelled against centuries of inferior cooking standards and are increasingly demanding better food — the restaurant trade, other than in the sheer number of establishments on offer, has not changed that much. Wages at the bottom are atrocious, and while a head chef in a major restaurant can be looking at a salary in the upper five figures or better, this is of little consolation to a commis or demi whose £12,000 – £14,000 a year would barely register on the economic consciousness of one of his peers in the City, raking in ten times as much for shuffling digits on a screen. Yet the one change apparent in the last decade or so has been a new influx of middle-class chefs. Many of today's stars — Alastair Little, Rowley Leigh, Jake Hodges — have a background far more 'privileged' than the majority of those among whom they work. The Oxbridge accent is no longer restricted to the customers.

It's harder to start out in London as a chef than it is anywhere else. You go into a kitchen and you're right in the deep end. About 50 per cent of chefs now probably started out somewhere local, a pretty basic kitchen that they could settle into. My junior sous chef started out at Harvester. And I started out nowhere special, but I loved it. But it's hard for a commis: they have to realise what they want to do and go for it. A lot stay because they like the atmosphere — sometimes they're too young to realise the hours they are doing. They come to work, have the laughs, see all the problems, the madness and think it's all really funny. Then they get nervous when the chef yells at them. But after work they can go out and stand around with lads who've been in the trade for five to ten years, oh yeah! At home, their mates are working on a building site, nine to five, same job every day, no pay rises. But they come into a kitchen, meet different people, see so many situations, have a laugh. That's why I think most of them stay in the trade: the atmosphere.

To want to stay in the business past being a commis, that depends, for example, on what the social life's like. There's a difference between a commis in the country and one in London. The country commis is part of a small brigade, probably working doubles, always in the kitchen, doing something they want to do, inspired by the food, and they're involved in everything because of the small staff. City commis get scared because the place is big, there's a lot of people in the kitchen, they don't know what's going on, they are trying to learn. So many commis turn to drugs and drink in London. There's a fair few commis come through, but not enough of them. I employ more demi chefs de partie than commis. You never really see a commis. They want to come into the trade on a better wage than they should be on. A lot of companies are now setting up apprentice schemes, giving the staff three to four years moving around their own restaurants. And then it all depends on how professional the restaurant and kitchen staff are towards them. If they're inspired, they'll stay. We've got ten apprentices at Groupe Chez Gérard. Look how big London is, how many restaurants there are. They stay for two years and move round the three restaurants. If they stick out the two years, then the dedication's there, they want to do it. And by then at least they understand it's not an easy life, that they won't get pampered, won't be working nine to five. You've got to get the work out of them – you are paying them. And they get used to that. But as apprentices they're not part of the hierarchy proper. They're doing the job, but also doing the college work and getting sent to the fish markets, and, for example, in a few weeks' time they're going to work in the bakery that delivers our bread, ten p.m. to six a.m. So they can get the theory and see how things are supplied and how things are made. And they'll go round and see everything. But once they've finished their apprenticeship and are up to demi chef de partie they won't go on any more courses.

I don't know why we're getting middle-class boys coming into the trade. They see it, hear about it, it's creative and they want to get into it. They're bored, want to do something different in life. There's a school been set up by two elderly women just outside London. You pay £1,500 to go there on a course – I think it's about six weeks – to learn how to be a chef. Then they try and get you an apprenticeship in a good restaurant. But who can afford to pay the course fee? Only the middle classes or the rich. You might ask, with their background, can they cope with it: in a kitchen on a Saturday night, getting shit chucked at them, specially as apprentices, being paid £120 a week? If they can adapt to that, the drive must be there.

You've got to work hard at the beginning to get to the top. When you do get to the top it will definitely pay – and if you're working hard and the restaurant's doing well you'll be up for bonuses. Keeping your staff even for a few weeks is hard, but I've kept mine for three months and upwards. I brought in about eight new faces, but they're good ones who want to stay. Last year they all wanted to leave, or left every few weeks because they couldn't do it. You basically spend one to two years at every level

— that's what I did. The fast track? Go and work in a restaurant with four staff. Start as a commis, get promoted to chef de partie because you know the kitchen inside out, know the menu, promotion's easy then. By the time you're twenty-one you could be head chef. But at the same time I could find you fifteen guys the same age as me who are still chef de parties or sous chefs. You can't go very far in a kitchen without brains. I know that in two years' time I would like to be looking at an average wage of fifty grand. I might be the head chef, but I've got to improve all the time. I've been here a couple of years now and all that time I've been changing the menus four times a year and undoubtedly improving myself. I have to do this because people below me want to see me doing something good. And that in turn will drive them to put more effort into what they do and for their futures.

WOMEN CHEFS

There's not a lot of girls in the industry. There are not enough women chefs. Though as far as I can see, women chefs in kitchens can be just as good as men. To me, whether it's a girl or a boy in the kitchen makes no difference as long as they're doing their job. I don't often get applications from girls, and when I go to an agency I don't particularly look for girls. But it comes down to the same thing for everyone; it's a case of if they can do the job they can have it, regardless of sex. At Billesley Manor there was a girl in the kitchen — nose always up in the air. She thought she was something special. So I used to really get on to her (which would have been the same if it'd been a male), 'What's this crap? What's that? Move this. Move that.' She ended up going off to the chef crying, saying I was picking on her. It wasn't because she was female, but because of her attitude. If you've got a job in a kitchen, darling, you've got to work just as hard as everybody else. But they've got a lot to prove – or they feel that way, working in a kitchen full of rude remarks and crude gestures all day long. It's a tough place to work, whatever sex you are. And the other thing is that being a chef is a physically hard job and not all women can do it. But those who can, they're fine. Most of the women chefs I've known, they really keep themselves together. One of the best chefs de partie at Quag's was a girl, she was brilliant. So quick, competent. Little stick of an Irish girl. Most of the female chefs I know are pastry chefs. Maybe it's the artistry of it that suits them.

There's no discrimination when it comes to promotion, but I think a lot of women feel there is. They feel it more than the blokes do. If a restaurant has a top sous chef, female, and an average sous chef, male, they'd take the female any day. If I had a kitchen full of women, and they were ugly, but they could cook – fine. If they're good-looking and they can cook, that's a bonus. But when you're in there working hard, sex doesn't come into it. The girls stink worse than the fellas at the end of the night on a busy service. If you've got a really good girl, say on the sauce section, after a busy service she'll go off and have a pint – not a glass of wine or half of lager. So it's not so much discrimination, as just not enough females in the trade. Having said that, when you take a good look there are plenty of women out there working, there's plenty of young commis and chefs de partie – but the majority of the celebrity chefs are men. There's only a few women chefs that are in the limelight; only so many of them that are in the top jobs and have their own restaurants and are successful. Everyone knows Rose Gray and Ruth Rogers at the River Café, or Sally Clarke at her restaurant, but after that . . .

Minorities — blacks, gays, whatever — basically don't have problems in a kitchen. Everyone gives as good as they get. Kitchen talk is pretty basic: what's happened the day before, who's shagging who, is she a moose, is she nice? There's a lot of humour that goes with it. With the gays, I think they're more relaxed if everyone knows they're gay. There were two on pastry at Gleneagles. To me it wasn't a big issue, I wasn't bothered about it. If the bigger boys got at them, I'd join in, but it wasn't a big deal for me. There was a gay chef de partie at Quag's — he didn't announce it, you sort of knew — and he had to bear the brunt of the gay jokes in the kitchen. It was just tough shit on him if he heard us talking about faggots.

CHAPTER FOUR
KITCHEN PORTERS

In the hierarchy of the kitchen, the KP, or kitchen porter, is the lowest of the low. Primarily a washer up, whether of the plates, bowls, knives and forks from the restaurant, or at the potwash, keeping abreast of the constant flow of used saucepans and frying pans coming from the chefs, his is a menial role. He may aspire to the low-level cooking tasks – preparing vegetables, washing salad, squeezing fruit for juices – and even, albeit rarely, join the brigade proper, but in the end it is not a job to be envied. His weekly wage barely surpasses the lunching bills of those whose leftovers (if he doesn't eat them himself) he scrapes into the pigswill bin. He is the butt of kitchen jokes, the ultimate in unskilled labour. Yet without a KP a kitchen could not function. His role is one not without respect.

There's quite a lot of people behind the scenes when you work in a kitchen, before the food gets to the table. You start with the kitchen porter, who's as important as the chef in my eyes. Although they're at the bottom of the hierarchy they get paid a good rate: anything between £4.50 and £6 an hour. A commis gets the same, the difference being, of course, that the commis will get better and better and can rise up the ladder, whereas the kitchen porter might stay there for ever. My head kitchen porter earns a good wage. He puts the hours in though, he earns his money. He's there at seven a.m. when I get there. He puts all the goods away. He preps all the veg, does the lemons for the pastry chef, does all the juicing, the grating of Parmesan, the citrus fruit. He's really involved in it. If I try to put the goods away before he gets there, he'll argue that he's the kitchen porter and I'm the chef and I shouldn't do it. People like him are gold dust. One of him in your kitchen, you're lucky. He works till the last minute in the day, then goes home, relaxes, forgets all about it. But he works so hard when he's in the kitchen.

At the Soho Brewing Company I employed two KPs and they worked seven days a week – six days with one working a double. They got paid by the hour. One of them was earning £350–400 some weeks. That was my mistake, I didn't realise how much they were likely to earn. They were getting nearly as much as the sous chef. They got very argumentative and cocky. So we lost them and brought in two lads who were from university who just wanted work for four months. They loved it. When I got to Soho Soho the KPs tried to spoof me, 'We can only do this, we have to do this that way, we can only do these hours.' I wasn't impressed: we got rid of those lousy porters and now we've got really good ones.

We use two KPs: the pot-washer, who works at a sink on the other side of the pass, and the plate man, who's in the corner at a big sink and does the plates, puts them all through the machine. The pot-washer has to do his job by hand. For the plate man there's a high-pressure tap to wash food off the plates before they go in the machine. A lot of places don't scrape the food into pigswill bins, they put it down the sink and one of those waste-disposal machines minces it up. Back at Gleneagles, where there were several restaurants, there'd be about 1,500–2,500 plates a day going to be washed in the machine. The sinks there were deeper than I'd ever seen before: really huge, not just normal pot-washing sinks. The lads working on potwash every night would work harder than anybody else in the building. All the food went down into a little gulley and got washed away when someone pressed the button, and at the end it reached a grinder and then off down the drain. So no pigswill at all there. But obviously in a kitchen like ours – our whole kitchen's about the size of the potwash section at Gleneagles – there's no room for something like that. That was such a big place there was a separate room for everything, for instance the silver – trays, knives, forks, spoons and so on – went through one machine, was passed through to the staff when it was dry and they stood there polishing day in, day out.

The KPs come in at nine a.m. for nine-thirty. They don't really have anything to do till then. If they come in too early they'll be walking round doing sod all, getting paid for it. You think they must be mad. Standing there doing dishes all day. There's gotta be something wrong with them. But you need them and I give as much respect to them as I do to the chefs.

Finding a good KP is not easy. We're in the situation now that when we get them we *know* that most of them are going to be useless. We had one the other week, he only lasted two days, and that was him gone. Another one, from some far-off African country, fifty years old, worked for me five to six weeks, came to work in a suit. I felt sorry for him – here he is, only ten years younger than my dad and he's washing pots and pans for me. But he didn't have the intelligence to keep the plate stacks all tidy, to put the plastic containers in the right place. He couldn't keep the floor clean, came in late, was slow, couldn't peel veg properly or quickly. So eventually I asked him to leave. I felt bad because he said, 'I'm really sorry, I'm not good enough for you, I know that. I'm going back to Uganda anyway.' And he left, really polite. I sent his wages off to him. Then three weeks later I got a postcard from him in Uganda, still apologising for not being good enough. 'If you come to Uganda with your family, come and stay for free, we'll look after you. Thank you for letting me work for you for five weeks.'

There might still be a few places now like Orwell described in *Down and Out in Paris and London*, but they'd be the ones owned by one person. In Orwell's day even chefs were treated badly. The head chef was God then, with hundreds of chefs scurrying round for the Master. They were under pressure and in turn put pressure on the KPs. But KPs, if the kitchens I've been in are anything to go by, are generally a crazy lot.

When I was at the Woodhey at Ellesmere Port, my first job in a kitchen, the kitchen porters were two old women, Millie and May. Absolutely fascinating, really funny, made you tea all the time, non-stop. They were on the pots and pans and the plate-washing machine all day long. No one could go near the pot-washing area, that was *their* area. They were about fifty, so tough, just loved the job. And they were always feeding the chefs. 'We're looking after our boys.' They didn't get paid much, but they did a good job. One of them had been a washer-up in a school for years and she'd looked after the kids. She loved working in the kitchen with us. Those two were like your second mum, the way they looked after you. You'd never have to shout at them. But there were things they couldn't do: they couldn't take the pigswill bins out, the way the KPs do here; we'd have to do that for them. And one day Millie came screaming out of the fridge, saying there was a mouse in there. When we looked, she'd knocked over some grapes on to the floor. That was her mouse: a little bunch of grapes. She was going mental, wouldn't work the rest of that day, went home in shock. She wouldn't believe it had been a grape not a mouse. When I moved on to the Regency we had a family where the sons used to help out as KPs, and we had the parents too. We used to call them the Clampitts, the Ellesmere Port hillbillies. The mother looked like Olive in *On the Buses*, with her hair all tied back. The father looked like a little Buddy Holly – always into his Elvis music. On their day off they did the flea market. Probably were gyppos.

At Gleneagles the KPs were from around Glasgow and Edinburgh; they were real ruffians, you felt it was the only job they could get. One bloke, he'd been there for years, an absolute nutter. He used to walk round tutting, tut-tut-tut all day long. If you asked him to do something, he'd just look at you, talking to himself all the time, and walk off. The sous chefs took the piss out of him. Go and get me some salmon lips, they'd say, or get me some chopped flour.

The sous chefs were meanest to Sammy, the nuttiest of them all. They stood him in the sink, put a bucket on his head and made him sing 'Tie a yellow ribbon round the old oak tree,' in front of the whole kitchen. They just laughed at him. He took it on the chin on the day, pretended not to care, but I bet he did. Though he was so simple I'm not sure whether half the time he actually realised they were taking the piss. You'd come down at breakfast time and he'd be sitting there with eight Weetabix on his plate, piling milk on top, talking to his breakfast bowl. But I suppose for him it was all right: free food, got paid, had somewhere to live.

The other KPs at Gleneagles all came from the rough parts of Glasgow and couldn't get another job. Most had scars all over their faces and all they talked about was the battles they'd been in. If there was trouble, out would come the bare knuckles. They had a great time, knew they were on a good number. They worked the hours, did the job, then out. They spent their money on nightclubs and women. And after work they could mingle with the chefs and management if they wanted because they were in the same accommodation. They could use all the sports facilities there too. They'd hire golf equipment and off they'd go. And some of them actually made it as chefs. There was one, Angus, and he just bothered people for a long time, 'I wanna be a chef, wanna be a chef.' Eventually they gave him a day's work in the kitchen – he did all right. So they chucked him straight on the veg section for three months. But he did well, learnt well. The other KPs took the piss out of him for working in the kitchen, aspiring to be a chef. I heard a couple of years later that he was doing really well in a kitchen. But most of the others, there was nothing else for them to do in Glasgow. And I think there was a waiting list to get a KP job at Gleneagles. There was so much went with the job, it was a brilliant deal. Some of them had been there for years.

At Billesley Manor there were five different KPs. The first two were called Spud and Trout. Spud wore a white boiler suit to work – always too small for him – and he was fat, looked like a spud. He was really strange, lived with his dad, and his dad lived with his dog. They spent all their money in arcades in Stratford-upon-Avon every day. Again, he was the butt of all the jokes, got all the abuse, all the shit. He'd give it all back though. He'd cry while you were giving him grief, he was a bit of a wimp. Then there was Trout, who worked opposite him. He looked like a trout – all these spots under his chin. He was terrible, a sight. He'd worked there for a year or so, he was a really hard worker. I was about twenty-one, twenty-two, but there was a sixteen-year-old chef there and he laid into these two all the time. He was a big lad. But they wouldn't say boo to people. They lived in the town, not very good family backgrounds, not enough intelligence to get even a factory job, just enough to be able to wash up.

Then there was Simon. He *was* Ronnie Corbett. About thirty-five, maybe forty. So brainy it was outrageous. Tiny bloke, four foot tall, about six stone. Wore the leeriest trousers, the worst clothes. He was so insecure. Lived in the smallest room at Billesley. His parents lived up the road, but he lived there. He'd have nervous breakdowns in the middle of a busy service or when he was in trouble. The chef used to ask him what motorway he had his breakdown on – really used to take the piss out of him. They'd find him lying in the staffroom on his back, like a little dying ant. He'd just collapse and have a fit. It was a bit sad but it was funny. You'd be working away, shouting, 'Simon! I need this, I need that.' And there he was, lying on the floor, collapsed. Pots and pans all over the kitchen, waiting to be washed and you'd have to pick him up, sit him down and give him a coffee until he settled down. One night he did it three times. We were so busy and he couldn't hack it. He was a nightmare. He was the worst KP I've ever known. But you couldn't sack him, he was just a good bloke. Sometimes he'd lock himself in his room, couldn't come out to do his job. Then you'd get his parents down to sort him out. He'd come up to you when you're really busy and start this; 'Did you know . . . did you know . . . did you know . . .?' 'Simon, fuck off! Wash the pans.' 'Yes, yes, no problem.' And he'd start washing up. Then he'd come back, hands on hips, 'Chef, did you know . . .?' Apparently what had happened was that he'd been under so much pressure doing his A levels that he'd tried to commit suicide and never been the same again. He'd boast about his driving lessons, 'I got up to ten miles an hour last week, did you know that?' So thrilled. We used to tease him. One day we told him; 'Simon, there's a fire!' He ran to the other end of the kitchen, got the extinguisher and let it off in the kitchen. A real nutter.

Then Billesley Manor decided to employ two more KPs, brought from a rehabilitation centre for alcoholics, from Glasgow. One of them started on the Saturday – train fare paid from Glasgow – got his room, all meals provided, so much an hour for doing his job, about £120 a week, not bad for then. He got something to eat, really quiet, never spoke to anybody, just got on with his work. We couldn't understand his Glasgow accent. Four days later we found out it was his twenty-first birthday, but that night he was washing up. Two weeks later he got his first wage packet, invited us all to his room and there's a crate of Castlemaine which he's giving to everybody. You realised he was saying, 'I used to be an alcoholic but I've come down to Stratford-upon-Avon to wash up and get myself a decent job, sort myself out.' Puts a can in the bin, opens another one. 'I think I'm gonna do really well here . . .'

Another lad came down from Liverpool. He was black, the only black in Stratford at the time just about. His first day shopping in Stratford he got nicked three times for shoplifting. He hadn't nicked anything, but he thought, 'Oh well, I'm the only black around, that's why they're picking on me.' He was a bit of a character. A big lad.

Then they brought back this other lad, Alan, six foot, grey hair, orange boiler suit for washing up in. He just turned up one day. The chef needed another porter and took him on. Alan lived in Birmingham and rode his bike from Brum to Stratford every shift. Breakfast shift, he had to start at six-thirty a.m., and he'd still come on his bike, a three-wheeler. He wore this boiler suit, bleached blond hair, had a stupid Brum accent, worst I've ever heard. Another nutter. His part-time income was from nude modelling and donating to the sperm bank. The chef sacked him one Sunday afternoon, about one p.m. – he'd had enough. Alan said, 'Can I finish me shift, please?' He was that stupid, he stayed to finish working through a busy Sunday lunch. After breakfasts, if the staff didn't want the leftovers, he took the whole lot on one plate – just *so* much food – then come lunchtime he'd be scraping food off all the plates to eat when no one was looking.

Most of the KPs in London are foreign. Most of mine today are North Africans, Algerians: I suppose it's the only job they can get. Another place I worked they were all Africans there – from Ghana, the Ivory Coast, Algeria, Morocco. They were sort of shipped in all together and of course the wages they could get were very good compared with what they'd be on back home. There always seemed to be a supply: whoever was in charge of the KPs just brought some in when he needed them. I don't know where they lived. Sometimes they stayed all night: during service they'd be there washing pots and pans, then after the restaurant closed they'd clean up, drink a few cans of beer and then they'd just nap for a few hours until the night shift woke them up and they'd finish the cleaning early the next morning.

At Odette's there were only two KPs, both Algerian. They worked seven days a week non-stop. They both drank. One worked night times. He was good and clean, but stupid, a dumbo. The other one did all the morning shifts and helped with the fish prep. His problem was that his feet stank. Everyone would make comments about it and he'd get upset and start a fight. The two Algerians had been there a while, then one decided to leave and we had to replace them both. We got a German girl, working nights. She was the biggest scavenger going. She took things home from the bin – bread, half a steak, ice-cream, cheeses. One day she bought a carpet and stored it out in the yard. When she was leaving, she went to pick it up – maggots everywhere. Obviously she'd got it from a dump. We had to bleach and do the whole kitchen out for about four hours. When she came in next day we sacked her straight away.

The KPs at Quag's were a mixture of Africans and Arabs. They were fighting all the time. That caused problems in the kitchen. Algerian KPs are very temperamental. Then you've got Ramadan. They prayed every four hours – most of them had a special mat in the changing room. We'd go up and say, 'Put in a word for West Ham on Saturday will ya?' They'd go mad. But those guys were the worst I've known in this trade for the arguments. Always arguing with each other, with the chef. 'Whose job that? Why should I do it? Why don't you do it? I'm not doing that. You're not Boss. Don't tell me what to do.' On and on and on. One day I asked this guy Alaji, as a good KP, to go round the back of the kitchen, pass one of the stocks for me. ('Passing' means pouring it through a strainer to get the clear liquid into another container.) He came back and I asked him where it was. 'I passed it for you,' he said. I went round the back of the kitchen, and he'd passed it for me from the brat pan, a big boiling pan. But where did he pass it? Down the drain. Worst nightmare I could ever have expected.

The KPs had to work really hard at Quag's. On a typical service there would be three KPs and a supervisor on the plate machine; two KPs on the hot wash; one KP brushing/mopping the floor, all night. And one KP polishing plates. In the daytime it'd be more or less the same team of people. One person all day would brush and mop the floor. Or sometimes he'd do the plates *and* the mopping. In the middle of a service at Quag's, all the chefs would have a deep tray in the corner of the section and as the pans were being used they'd be chucked into these deep trays. Every five or ten minutes they'd shout for a porter to collect the trays, and he'd run past the busy chefs, pick the tray up, take it out and bring a clean one back with him; then he'd take the tray to the potwash, the plunge they call it, and wash all these pots and pans. At the end of the night, as all the chefs were cleaning down, then the KPs would be responsible for all the rest, the blanching pots, the little sauce containers, the little frying pans. And they'd always have it done by half twelve, or about an hour after the chefs had finished. Then, when they finished, a team of KPs from a private company came in and blitzed the whole kitchen. So you could leave Quag's kitchen after doing 800 on a Saturday night and first thing Sunday morning you'd walk in and it would be spotless. This was a wonderful system to me: a KP just to polish plates, a KP just to mop the floor, a KP just to wash plates.

CHAPTER FIVE
SHIFTS AND ROTAS

Rotas, coming from the same root as the word rotation, are a vital and sometimes difficult task for chefs to work on. As most people work Monday to Friday nine to five this is seen as the normal working pattern. Most kitchens have to operate seven days a week for about eighteen hours a day and with the kitchen rotas you need to cover every section with staff. This is how it works.

Take a large London restaurant with fifty to sixty chefs, and six sections. On each section per service you need four sauce chefs, three grill chefs, two hot larder chefs, three crustacea chefs, four cold larder chefs and three pastry chefs. Now, as I've said, this is per shift, meaning lunch or dinner. In addition there will be at least three senior chefs to run the whole kitchen. If you work a lunch, that's one shift; if you work a dinner, that's also one shift, otherwise known as a 'straight' shift. Lunch and dinner on a single day is a 'double' shift. All chefs are employed to do six of these shifts over five days. So you'll do four 'straight' shifts and one 'double' shift. To staff the kitchen fully for every service you'd need to cover 266 shifts per week. That's about forty-four chefs per week. Then you've got four veg prep chefs and seven extra chefs to cover each section for holiday relief, sickness and days off. Then you have your six to eight senior chefs. It's vital that all these shifts are covered to ensure that the kitchen runs as smoothly as it can. The headaches start when chefs ring in sick. Then you have to start asking chefs to work overtime, or to work on their days off. If no one can cover the extra hours needed then you are in trouble, especially as you're going to serve 850 people dinner and 250 people lunch.

Staff shortages are actually growing, they're getting worse each day. Some restaurants can be up to ten full-time staff short a week. Which says to me straight away sixty shifts. Now you can only cover so many of those shifts with overtime before the staff get tired and pissed off. Not forgetting that possibly there could be chefs on holiday. This is the 'fuck me' stage. You're really in the shit now. And this is when it can start to affect the food because, unless you keep them motivated, people are going to stop caring and look for a job elsewhere. I can remember sitting up at home until three in the morning trying to do the rotas for all six sections. It's the easiest thing in the world when you have a full brigade, but the worst when you're short.

Most kitchens, especially those owned by companies, employ chefs on a basic six shifts per week. That's on your contract. Some privately owned kitchens work on minimal staff and the chefs end up working 'afd': all fucking day. Five to six days a week. This is what it used to be like years ago. In small country-house hotels you'll work eight hours, four hours in the morning and four hours at night. What attracted me to London was the four straights and one double idea. Wherever you go, though, the system is the same: that means you'll always need to employ enough staff to cover every section. When I was at Odette's although we had five sections we never had ten chefs; there were only the five of us working 'afd' five to six days a week. All the boys there, including the chef, did this. In each other's faces, in a small kitchen, for three years. Your only social life was on Friday and Saturday, after midnight. And Sunday. This was when all your money went, but once Monday morning came around you were back in the kitchen feeling like a bag of hungover shit and facing those buckets full of fish to fillet. At times like this relationships are best avoided. When you've worked five to six shifts week in, week out, the last thing you need to hear is somebody whingeing and not understanding why you don't drop your knives in an instant to listen, so they can nag you to death. And, to be honest, you're more interested in the food.

The advantage of a brigade like the one we had at Odette's is that you all know exactly how everything works, so you can swap sections every week. I'll never forget though, come six o'clock at night, whilst waiting for the first check to come on, you'd find the chefs sleeping on the benches, floors, by the warm ovens in the winter, in the dry stores and the backyard in the summer. Those fifteen-hour days were always long and you grabbed your sleep whenever or wherever possible.

Talking about the actual hours, in a large restaurant (and most others) a lunch shift should be from eight a.m. to four p.m., dinner from four p.m. to midnight. A double would be both shifts together with a break between three and five in the afternoon, but in my experience it never happened. The only safe shift to do was a dinner. You always started on time and were out half an hour after closing. If you were on a lunch shift, getting in at eight a.m. was easy, but expecting to go home at four-thirty was silly. Of course when there's extra back-up prep to be done, it's good to stay till it's all complete. The problem is, though, that there are bad chefs who keep the sous chefs back till seven or eight o'clock just for the hell of it. Imagine what it was like when special evenings had been booked and I had a head chef who made me feel as if I should never arrange anything in the evening after a lunch shift. The worst shift pattern you could have was — going on my own experience — a dinner shift (Friday), double shift (Saturday) and lunch shift (Sunday). Living where I did the timetable was as follows: start work Friday at three p.m., finish Friday night at one-thirty a.m.; night bus home, get home at three a.m.; up Saturday morning at five-fifteen, back in work by seven; finish seventeen-hour shift around one-thirty a.m. Saturday night; same bus and sleep as Friday night and back up at six-fifteen on Sunday morning. Then into work till five that evening. Physically these three days were far more demanding than the effort of simply cooking food. It was the adrenalin that kept you going. I wasn't on my own then — there were plenty of chefs doing the same hours and it probably gets worse in other places. I can understand a brigade which has to work untold hours for perfection with a master chef, but not one working untold long hours for no apparent reason in an ordinary kitchen.

In my own brigade of twenty, at the moment I am fully staffed and have every shift and section covered. I am also aware that if half of them walk out tomorrow I'd be up till three a.m. doing more than just rotas. I doubt that would happen though: a chef who has no respect for staff . . . has no staff.

CHAPTER SIX
RECRUITMENT AND LEARNING

If you take in every level of public eating place, from Michelin-starred palaces of *haute cuisine* down to the meanest, least appetising greasy spoon, and add in cafés, pubs – offering anything from traditional (and barely edible) 'pub grub' to gastro-pubs offering sophisticated menus which echo their larger, smarter cousins – the burgeoning chains like Café Rouge, and the vast range of sandwich bars and similar 'snackeries', there are perhaps 100,000 'restaurants' in London. The current *Time Out Guide to Eating and Drinking* indexes around 2,300 places worthy of a good night out. Out of all of these, what might be termed the 'top-level' restaurants number around 1,000, and range in their turn from merely 'good' to egregiously 'excellent'. And all of them, irrespective of quality, have a single unifying problem: there are never enough chefs (or, indeed, waiting staff) to go round. However good a kitchen may be, there are almost invariably two or three chefs too few on any given day. Sometimes they're ill, sometimes on holiday, but most often the talent simply isn't available. A good head chef bargains for the shortfall – he has little choice – but it's another strain on an already stressful environment.

There must be 30,000 catering vacancies in London on any one day. That goes from a trainee chef, a waitress, a kitchen porter, from commis to sous chef. When someone takes one job, they're leaving somewhere else to go to it, so there's still a vacancy. People can't get the staff – there's not 30,000 catering staff out there looking for work. And, after all, if they are good chefs, why are they out of work? The young ones won't take the jobs, or can't afford to, because they've moved to London, and the pay they're offered means that they can't afford to live and work. Most young chefs come from within the London area so they can live with their parents and travel in. They earn £8,000 to £10,000 when they're training, so they need their parents' support. If they don't have that, they have to find somewhere to live. There's the PM Club in Earls Court. It's like a big hostel that provides accommodation for chefs new to the London scene. A lot of hotel staff are given accommodation before they arrive in London, but restaurant staff don't get looked after as well as this. So this is where the PM club comes in handy, the only snag being that there's a waiting list and it will probably cost half your wages to stay there.

It's very rarely you've got all the chefs you should have. You're nearly always down, even in the top restaurants. When I was at Quaglino's we were seven chefs down every week. That's just one restaurant. There should have been fifty-seven chefs. We had fifty. The last time I dropped in there, in August 1999, they were fourteen chefs down. Not long ago, at a friend's restaurant, they were six chefs down. He's not going to get six chefs for a place like that instantly. Today a lot of chefs want to go out as well. They want to work, but they want to go out, and if you go out in London, £60 won't last you a night if you want to have a really good time. That's why it's difficult to get commis chefs in

London. People simply won't work for the money. And if you can't fill the vacancies for junior/commis chefs, who are you going to find to fill the chef de partie vacancies — because there are no commis chefs coming through the ranks to end up as chefs de partie.

Dotted all over you've got agencies for restaurant staff. The recruitment agencies obviously grow as the industry grows and they know there's plenty of money out there to be made on chefs. They're like bounty hunters in a way, going out to catch someone and deliver him or her for the fee involved. If you're not working on word of mouth, then that's how you recruit. I had never used a recruitment agency myself before 1995, when I decided to leave Odette's. I knew I wanted to leave so I gave thirteen weeks' notice, which was like a fair bit of notice, to the chef and said I'll be leaving on a certain date, because it was time for me to move on. Now this was quite strange and new territory for me because I'd never used an employment agency before, apart from the Ellesmere Port Job Centre to get a job at Gleneagles. I just walked into an agency one day and went, 'My name's Andrew Parkinson. I'm looking for a job. I've worked at so and so for three years, here's my background, what can you do for me?' And this girl looks at me and says, 'Wow, gold!' She took me into an office and then you just fill a form out and they talk to you for half an hour. They get to know you because then, when they've got to know you, they're going to sell you to all these different chefs and try to send you out to as many places as possible.

She knew from what I've done that I've got a good background. Basically she knew that it wasn't going to take her a long time to find me a job. I could see her thinking, here's a good 10 per cent. So she talked to me for half an hour, got me to fill the form out, listened to what I said, blah blah blah, and then she thought, 'I'll be ringing someone straight away.' It's in her interests to get me a job. Of course, she always takes people's details, but often she knows they're not really up to it. When someone like myself comes along, who's had some top-class experience, it must be their lucky day.

An agency takes at least 10 per cent of your first year's wages. They get a one-off payment, I think after the first three months. The chef works a probationary period, and then when that's completed the recruitment agency will invoice the company for their 10 per cent. It's good business for them but it makes it expensive for personnel departments in the restaurant companies. Of course they've got a choice, but there's a general belief that if they go through an agency they're going to get better people. They can advertise in the *Evening Standard* and it will cost them £1,500 for one advertisement. On that basis, if they get three decent chefs out of it, then it's only cost them £1,500. *If* they get three decent chefs. Alternatively they can use the recruitment agency and employ three people and that's going to cost them £4,500. So on a purely financial basis it's cheaper to go through the newspapers or to talk to people you know (which costs nothing after all), but you're not going to get the quality that you get through a good agency which knows its clients.

Years ago when you first got a job in catering you mainly went to college, you did a lot of written work, a lot of theory and that was that. Now and again at night time you did the cooking for people coming into the restaurant where you worked. But not often. Then you got your qualifications and went to work in hotels or restaurants. That's the way it was done. Now you get places like the Apprentice Chef School down by Tower Bridge, in Butler's Wharf. These courses cost money, and if, say, you're the manager of a bookshop and you decide you want to be a chef, you have to find the money yourself. But in many cases the people who go are already working for a restaurant and get sent there by their company. And in that case the company pays the fees. The idea, if you're already working four days a week in a proper kitchen, is that you get taught theory and useful skills like filleting fish. Whoever's paying the fees, what the apprentice wants is theory: written work involving courses on stock control, basic receipes, health and hygiene and weights and measures. He wants to learn stuff he's not going to get starting out as a commis. The reality is often that you do cooking, and punters turn up, as in any restaurant, and pay for it. If that is what's going on, and someone's making money out of it, then it's a clever little scheme.

Going back a century, kitchen work was probably just as tough – but for different reasons. You'd learn the trade off tough masters, on little money, and have to train for years just to get a commis chef's job. But after that, when you went for a job, you were qualified. But now, as head chef, you often have to take people on who haven't had anything like that level of training. I'm lucky at the moment, I've got a full team. I do my own recruitment, and make sure I'm bringing the right people in. At Soho Soho I need twenty chefs. Since I've been here, twelve people have left. Four I was happy to see go and eight were told to get out and never come back. I've completely changed my kitchen brigade upstairs, always by bringing in someone good. It's a case of waiting for someone bad to leave so I can bring in someone good. Downstairs too I've been lucky to get rid of most of the bad people and bring in good people. Most of my staff come from an agency around the corner. The guys who run it were in the trade themselves, chefs for a couple of top London soccer clubs, which wasn't too bad, but in the end they got out – probably for the same reasons most chefs do: long hours, not enough money. Now they know that they can provide chefs for the industry and offer them work in places that won't put them off the career. To do this they make sure they have as much information as possible on the person whose talents they're selling, plus they know about what sort of chef runs every kitchen, so that they can make sure they find the right sort of kitchen for you and supply the kitchen with the right sort of chef. They're good, and a lot of agencies are, but not all recruitment agencies cut the mustard. Some just see you as 10 per cent, not as a person, and when they think like that they can actually ruin your career . . .

Temps are doing well in London at the moment because there's such a shortage of trained staff. A lot of people in the trade have left permanent jobs to become temps because they then get cash in hand. A friend of mine worked at the Royal Lancaster for about eight years, had enough and went to an agency. Now he works in manor houses. They're doing hourly work, not having to think, just to do. Plenty of restaurants use temp staff. You'll get temps who've been in the trade five or six years, but they'd rather temp in different places all over and get paid cash in hand. They do pay a penalty, however. They can't buy a house or do other things because they haven't got a full-time job. And when they do decide to get back into a kitchen from temping, they're going to be a bit far behind. If someone comes to me and says, 'I've been temping for five years, and now I want to get back into full-time work,' I'll say no. How do I know he won't disappear after three months, when I've paid £3,000 for him from an agency?

The year I arrived at Soho Soho £8,000 was paid out on temp

staff in three months. They're not dedicated to the company, to the hours they're doing, or to you. They're just doing the work, getting a fast buck, getting out. If they're chef de partie level they'll get £7–8 an hour. A sous chef, £10 an hour. More per hour than full-time staff, whose pay is calculated by shift (they get overtime on top). But it's an insult to the kitchen staff working next to temps who are getting more money and saying; 'No, I can't work Friday, I'm off, can't work Saturday, I'm off.' But gradually I knocked them all down, and by January, my second month, I'd got rid of them all and haven't used a temp since. I refuse to use a temp. Firstly, I don't really need to. I've got a good staff who'll always offer to work extra. We can be one short, but it can still go well because we're organised. If someone's there who can run the sauce and we're short, I'll let them do the sauce, but if no sauce boys are there, I'll have to do it. But before we changed things, if they were short one night, they'd ring an agency straight away. Now, because I've got a good team together, and I treat 'em well, we get it all organised, and I don't really have a problem when we're short. Someone will say, 'I'll do an extra shift.' I've made a difference in that respect.

I hire and fire my own staff. In accordance with the law, when employing people, each and every person has to be asked, 'Have you got a passport, visas, work permits, etc? Have you worked in a kitchen before? Do you have to work afternoons because of college in the morning or vice-versa? Well, come and do a day's work for me tomorrow, we'll see what you're like.' If after two weeks they're shit, that's it, if they last three weeks you'll probably keep them a long time.

Take this boy I had in a few months ago. He's typical. Down from the Midlands, looking for a job in London. He rings a few agencies in London, gets to know them, hits one he likes and they say, 'Come down to London, we'll speak to you for an hour, we'll arrange some interviews, about six.' So he has his six interviews. They decide whether to invite him for a trial and he decides whether he wants to go. He might have said, 'I'll try all six.' He came to see me on the Friday when he got into London and stayed in the kitchen for about six hours. Someone like him will look round it, decide if he likes it, if the atmosphere's good, if he can get on with the chef, that it's a healthy establishment to work in. And the chef will decide whether he's got proper knife skills, if he's looking at the right things, if he's asking the right questions, if he feels the lad's committed to what he wants to do. Then the boy goes to the other places and sees what they're like. He'll make his own mind up. Money will be first on his list, then hours and shifts. In the event I never employed the boy from the Midlands because luckily one of my boys, who I thought was going to leave, actually stayed. It is easier for me to promote from within, knowing I've promoted properly, and then get myself a commis chef I can train up from scratch, rather than bring someone in at a higher level, spend a lot of recruitment money on him, and then no one else gets promoted.

That boy would have got a job. Probably he was offered the other five. He wanted to be a chef de partie. He's from Birmingham, he's twenty-eight – a bit old, but then he's been in Birmingham. Now he's come to London, and it's tougher to hold your own here than it is in Birmingham. I offered him £15,000, a few other places would offer perhaps £16,000 to £17,000. I didn't offer him a job, just said how much we'd pay him. He was good enough to be offered a job by me. But I thought, 'If I employ him and this other chap doesn't leave, I'm overloaded.' So I've got to take the gamble that the boy who's already here will stay.

On the other hand there's a lot of times you just go on word of mouth. If you know of someone who's looking for a job, you've saved the recruitment money you'd be paying to the agency. They probably paid about five grand or so for me, so they've got to make sure it's worth it. I got to Billesley Manor via the head chef: he invited me back for a trial. A trial shift is set up so the candidate can get a look at the kitchen, see how the brigade works and look at the overall organisation. He can see if the food spoken about in the interview is what it was advertised to be, whether or not he'd like to work in the brigade and whether there is room for promotion, just by looking at the skills of the rest of the brigade. It also works the other way. For instance I gave a trial to a chef de partie candidate a while ago and he couldn't make a *beurre noisette*. No way will he get a job from me. The candidate can tell you a load of bull, and you can see this as soon as he arrives half an hour late with his mum's knives. You're looking for more than just cooking skills. If someone comes for a day's trial and just does what I tell him and nothing else, I can see there's no initiative there. He's not helping others without being asked, not asking the right questions. So you can tell he's not for you. The bottom line is if I give them a job and they don't do it well, they're out on their arse. They get a thirteen-week trial. But you know after two weeks whether they'll fit in. That's twelve kitchen shifts for them to suss out how your kitchen works. Quite a long time.

I got into the Lancaster because one of my friends worked there. And then I got into Odette's through Steve, a really good friend who worked at Gleneagles with me. I went for an interview there, two minutes: 'Can you cook?' 'Yeah.' 'Right, you're in.' I worked with him for a night and he offered me the job before I left. I went from £11,000 to £13,500. I started a couple of weeks later. Straight in at the deep end. I walked into the kitchen, and there was no, 'This is how we do this, this is how we do that.' It was just; 'Right, there's the stove, you're on the sauce tonight.' You've got to do it straight away, and that's it. But the longer you work in the trade, the harder it gets, for one reason or another. At Quag's I had my trial on a busy service, 220 for lunch. I was in a kitchen where everybody knew what they're doing, using proper knives for the proper food. No using a boning knife to chop parsley, which I'd seen in other places. I was nervous when service came round. It was tough but the time flew by. Big buzz. I was shaking at the end of it, not through fear, but because I'd worked so hard.

My first real job was at Gleneagles. At the time I was out of a job, living at home, getting very drunk, thinking, 'What's it all leading to?' I'd been trying to get jobs in the area near my home as a chef de partie. But I lacked experience. I'd never been to college; I'd done a year's YTS – a few bits of written work here and there – and I'd worked in similar-style kitchens for three years. That was my experience. The division in the kitchen in those places was just starter, veg and main – no fish or sauce sections. Anyway, I tried to get chef de partie jobs in the Lake District – thank God I never got one, I could never have taken on a kitchen or organised anybody, I didn't know enough about food. Then I got the job in Scotland. I became a commis chef at Gleneagles. That changed my life, and it's why I'm doing what I am today. I got turned down when I first applied, because I didn't know Gleneagles was a five-star hotel, one of the best in the world. I just thought; 'Oh a five-star hotel in Scotland, must be quite nice.' They'd advertised in the job centre in Ellesmere Port and in Liverpool and the interviews were in Liverpool. David Cranston, the head chef, never sent anyone else out to do the interviewing of potential staff, he did it all himself.

He'd gone to the Ellesmere Port Job Centre, and they set up interviews for chefs. I'm sure everybody he interviewed that day was a fully qualified chef, but I just went along not knowing anything about it. The job was for a commis (a trainee) chef, working in a five-star kitchen with seventy-two other chefs. I went to the interview, and David Cranston showed me some of his menus and asked me what food I'd done. I told him I'd been working in these big places, doing these prawn cocktails and melon boats. I must have looked so silly in front of him. I had no qualifications, no chance of getting the job, a one-year HCITB training scheme behind me and three years in dinner-dance hotels. Eventually I got a letter saying the position wasn't for me. I thought, 'Well that's fine.' And I went to another interview at this naff place in Ellesmere Port, five and a half day shifts, £55 a week. I was about to take it, but I got a phone call – in my next door neighbour's because we didn't have a phone – David Cranston had called for me. And all these women, aunties and everything were sitting talking, laughing in the background. He said, 'There's a job available for you, when can you get here?' I told him to ring me back on the Monday night, I'd need to sort things out. I was really excited. I had to decide: do I want to go up there, or do I want to play snooker still? I'd just gone through to the next round of the Chester Cup. The decision was to drop my snooker, but on the Tuesday night I was travelling to Gleneagles with my snooker cue and knives in hand.

After Gleneagles the next jobs I got were all word of mouth until, when I left Odette's, I finally went to the recruitment agency and was sent to Quaglino's. That day they did 220 lunches, 140–150 of those were fish and I was on the fish section. It was all, 'Prep this, prep that.' When it came to lunch-time service, you'd finish off a few sauces, and they'd go, 'Right, this for that dish, this for that dish.' I just got hammered with checks. All I had to do was keep cooking and putting up the food as fast as they wanted it. At Odette's we'd do twenty-five for lunch, now I was doing 140. You're thrown in at the deep end. If I'd failed that trial day, I wouldn't have got the job. I knew I could cook, I wasn't scared of the cooking. What scares you is thinking, 'Are this lot a lot better than me? Can they do it better?' But you start working and the others look at you, 'Oh, he's doing all right.' You're cooking it the right way, not doing anything wrong, and you just make sure you keep doing your prep, getting your fish on in advance, and then when the checks are really hammering, just keep going. After the service I had a chat and that night I did the pass. I came back and did another shift. A lot of people just do one shift, but I said I wanted to do a whole day, I wanted to see everything. So I went on a break and my face was just covered in salt, with the heat and sweat and all. Then I went back and did the pass and they let me do it for half the night. I was getting things wrong, but people were helping me: 'Chef, do this, do that.' And when I walked away at the end of the day I thought: I hope I get the job. I was so overwhelmed by the whole day, just couldn't believe it. And I knew the chefs there were serious people, they were good boys. I'd been think-ing I'd done really well at Odette's. But now it was back to the beginning and you've got to get yourself sorted out, prove to people you can do it. There were a lot of senior chefs de partie at that restaurant, and they were all after the junior sous chef's job. They couldn't get a junior sous chef for a year, kept inter-viewing and interviewing, giving jobs to people who couldn't hack it. Then they gave me the job and they expected a lot from me. What drove me on was the people below me trying to catch me out, so I had to do it right and I really worked hard at it.

Specially in the first six months. But the organisation was so good, you just slotted in to what you were supposed to do.

At Quag's I became involved in the recruitment. I was sort of in charge of the recruitment from junior sous chef downwards. So I got to know about all the agencies and I began to make personal contacts. So when I wanted to leave it was easy enough to ring up someone and say, 'Look I really want to leave here, what can you do for me?' And they know me, they know where I'm working, they know what job I do, so they know a lot already before they even meet me. The job I wanted was a head chef or a senior sous, and the company I used was West One, who got me a job in R.K. Stanley, a new British sausage restaurant. British food, sausages and beer, and it was going to be the bee's knees, it was going to be the nuts, but from the first day I went in I was in doubt. Do I really want to do this? Do I want to work here? And it was a disaster. I had thought I was on to a right one and I thought it was all good, telling everybody that I was head chef, and I was featured in a magazine talking about our sausages, and it was all great and then all of a sudden it was just all wrong. I was there a very short time and I had to quit.

So here I was, stuck. It never hit home until I've gone to the agency, who got me the job there, and they're like, 'We're really sorry, we didn't realise it'd happen like this,' but what I didn't appreciate until later on was that everybody knew I probably wouldn't get on with the executive chef but nobody actually ever told me. So now I was just scraping by, doing part-time work, which was OK in the short run, keeping me alive, but I was wondering how my career was going to progress. Some days I'd get so frustrated that I'd pass a phone box and ring the agency up and ask, 'Have you got anything', pass the next phone box when I was walking round Romford, a ten-mile walk,

'Have you got anything? Has anybody rung yet? Have you got a number for me? Have you got this, have you got that?' And then it was, 'Well no, but we're trying. We're looking for you and we're doing our best. Something should come up soon and you will get the job that you want, and something's out there for you . . .', and all this palaver, this misery, went on for ages.

I felt screwed by the agency, but I didn't think they'd done it on purpose. They kept saying they'd get me some work, but they couldn't find the job I wanted. At the same time I'd been in touch with another agency, who suggested some part-time work, and while I was doing that they would find me the right job. So it was all about keeping me happy until they got me the right job. They got me a job at £10 an hour, working at Smollensky's in the Strand.

I went and met Michael Gottlieb, who was the boss. He asked me if I would go over to the Smollensky's Balloon in Dover Street. It was a good gig: I was getting paid £10 an hour and I had to work sixty hours a week, so I knew I was getting £600 a week. It was the easiest money I've earned. It wasn't the job I wanted, I knew that, but there wasn't anything else on offer, and I still had to think about the mortgage and all that palaver. So the next day I went to Smollensky's and spent two and a half weeks working there. I was going in at ten in the morning and finishing at ten at night, doing all the hours I had to do, making up my sixty hours. In the meantime, the recruitment agencies were still sending me to different restaurants, or meeting me again and saying would you like to go here or there's a chance for you to go and work there, or we've got some work lined up for you after Christmas. So here I am, doing my split shifts, and in between going off to the recruitment agency and speaking to the bloke for half an hour, really uptight: I've got to get back, got to do some more proper work.

The next thing was that the people who got me the job at Smollensky's offered me work at a restaurant in South London. This time the problem was the money. I was expecting a proper wage for the job, and the owner was paying me a commis's wage. When I found out I just walked, and the next morning I rang up the agency straight away and told them that I'd left and why. They went mad. They said ring her up now and explain to her why you walked out, so I said all right, I will. So I rang her up and she said, 'Andrew, I told you I was going to pay that much.' So I had a row with her on the phone. I rang the agency back up and said she's taking the piss, don't do that to me, so then we had a bit of a row too, and there I was – out of a job again.

After that I was offered work at Riccardo's in west London. This was part-time again. I'd go down to Riccardo's and get paid £50 for an hour's work and then I'd charge him £50 for doing consultancy work at home. So I was making a little bit of money, but then I got a letter from the taxman saying you've earned so much and you've got to pay tax on it and you've got to produce all these documents. So that one came to an end. Then I got yet another job and that didn't work either. Working in this place called the Cube, in Swiss Cottage. Again it was good money, but that was it. I was in this kitchen where everyone was just ordering bowls of chips. Chips, chips, chips and that was it. It was just this terrible six months: I'd left Quag's at the end of October and here I was in the middle of March. I'd had a series of jobs that hadn't worked out and now I've got the worst of the lot: a good wage package, but the worst possible job. I felt really desperate, but then I got a phone call from the recruitment agency that got me the work with Smollensky's. They sent me down to the Soho

Brewing Company to meet the owner and I took that job. It lasted six months, opening a new place, which was very hard, but what mattered was that it was what I wanted and the way I wanted it. Finally, when I was at Soho Brewing Company, this person from the agency rang up out of the blue, 'I haven't spoken to you for ages, how are you doing, what are your plans?' The human resources director at Groupe Chez Gérard had rung them looking for a head chef and a couple of sous chefs. So they rang me up and asked if I was interested in working for this group. Go along and meet so-and-so. Four interviews later, I thought, 'Yeah, I like the idea of this job.' And I took it and good times returned.

CHAPTER SEVEN
OPENING UP

It is arguable that, week in week out, more new restaurants open up in London than any other enterprise. They live or die for a variety of reasons, but the initial experience, the creation of the new establishment, and more particularly its kitchen and the decision on what food is to be served, are common to all. After a decade of gradual promotion through the kitchen ranks, and a less than encouraging six months in what he describes as a 'professional wilderness', Andrew was asked to open a brand-new restaurant, the Soho Brewing Company, situated in the heart of Covent Garden. All in all, he stayed there for six months before the management changed and he was head-hunted away to run a new restaurant.

In March 1998 I'd left Quaglino's, I'd been through a series of pretty unsatisfactory jobs, and I was still on the lookout for something better. The last thing I'd done was a day's trial at the Ivy, but that wasn't right, and I got this call from the agency. This chap who owned the Soho Brewing Company wanted to open a brand-new restaurant-cum-brewhouse which would serve good food and good beer all made in one place. It was German beer and they'd brought in an expert from Germany to oversee it. I wasn't their first choice – the first chef they'd talked to had decided to take the job. The first thing he did was to write out this menu, which really impressed Ewan, the chap who owned the company, and Mark, the manager. They thought, 'This menu's just what we want, a really really good menu. It'd match the beer.' Prices were kept quite low, which was good, because what you can't be doing is serving food at £20 a head when the beer's only £2 a pint. The trouble was that what he was after didn't work.

So they employ Andrew Parkinson: he's the new chef, and he has to match the food to the concept. The concept was great food, great beer, and that was that. All made in-house. So first of all you have a look at the size of the kitchen. It was half-built, but I'd seen the plans, and I knew what to expect. First thing they gave me the freedom to put the menu together, but the prices couldn't be too high – steak for £12, not higher.

The first thing I realised was that the previous chef's menu was far too big for where he was. He'd written it out before he'd seen the kitchen, before he knew what his wages budget was, before anything. And when you do that it never works. He couldn't have cooked that menu – he wouldn't have had the equipment, the chefs, the space or the time. My menu there was made to match the facilities and abilities of the staff I had, the number of staff I had, the amount of time I had to get it on the table. You can't just write out a menu based on what might be good to cook and eat, there are other important factors that you have to take into account, especially when you're starting up a new restaurant: equipment, chefs on duty, the amount of dishes you're going to have on the menu, the overall concept, the number of restaurant covers (i.e. seats) and the opening hours. All these things have to be taken into consideration.

The first thing you tackle is the equipment. Building a kitchen and fitting it out, you're looking at 50 per cent of your investment. If you don't buy the equipment, you can't cook the food to put on the table. Once I've seen the equipment I've got, then I can decide what the menu will be. When you design a kitchen, you've got to have in mind what you'll be doing in it. You think: everything in that section, I want to keep it warm, plates warm, have a bain-marie there to keep the sauces warm, because I'm gonna have to make a full bain-marie of sauces every service because we're going to be so busy. Instead of saying; 'No, I just want stoves there and that's it.' Or, 'We'll have a griddle, couple of good salamanders.' The design of all this equipment is just getting better and better. But at SBC I didn't have all that. There wasn't the room and there wasn't the budget. I wasn't able to get in on the design – it was more or less organised before I got there – and we fitted everything into the kitchen as well as we could. There was no hot lamp on the pass – the place where the food gets placed before the waiter takes it to the table; you should have a hot lamp to keep dishes warm. So we had to make sure the food that went up was straight off the grill, out of the oven, straight on the plate, on to the pass straight away. We had one chargriddle. We thought we'd use that for steaks and grilling fish. We had one small range, two hotplates, two small gas burners to put stock on, one hotplate for the plate itself and one fryer with two baskets. That was all the cooking equipment we had. Completely minimal. And the menu I wrote had to fit in with that equipment.

So here was this kitchen that wasn't big at all and we thought, 'What are we going to do? How are we going to build the menu?' It obviously wasn't going to be fine dining. There were people standing there drinking beer, being rowdy. We thought that if people were going to drink beer, they'd need something solid to go with it. If they were having wine, they'd want lighter food. But the main feature was beer, so we decided to develop a sausage to go with the beer, and a simple steak dish, fish and chips with a beer batter, a light starter menu with vegetarian choices and meat choices – black pudding, black and white pudding with caramelised apple that would go well with the beer. We had a pork dish with Thai spices to make it different from the steak dish. We had a *parfait* to contrast with the black pudding. We had beetroot salad and potatoes with horseradish. And all of this was based on the idea of making the menu match the beer.

Then there were the kitchen staff, the chefs. I was going to have one chef on the larder section, one on the pass and the sauce section, and one on the grill. Three chefs at a time. For 100 covers that's not a lot. So that's another factor in writing the menu. So when you get to the menu, you have to think about how many chefs are going to be able to cook it, how many covers at any one service, and how much prep you can have ready to go for a service. If you put twelve dishes on, it's going to be too much. Eight dishes is probably about right. You've got to have fish, meat and vegetarian, and in the starters you've got to have quite a lot of vegetarian really. If you put vegetarian dishes in your menu, it saves people asking, 'Oh, could you do something vegetarian?' Twenty years ago you wouldn't bother. But now a lot of people are concerned about what they eat, they want to look after themselves. So if you offer that choice, you'll get more people to eat there.

They gave me a budget of, I think, £112,000 a year, which included my wages. I could afford seven people. The previous chef had decided he was going to have twelve. I was given seven – five chefs, 2 KPs, which left me with a terribly small budget to pay staff. It was nothing compared to what I should have been given. But that's what you've got and it's not going to change and the next thing you have to look at is what you can afford, which means only so many chefs working at one time, and looking carefully at what goes in the menu. I had four staff to begin with: myself, my sous chef, the chef de partie, the commis chef. They worked with either a half or one day off for about six weeks when we were opening. We worked sixteen hours a day for six weeks to open the place. It only got better when we employed someone else. He'd worked for a couple of years as a commis chef, but although the workload in the kitchen lightened up he actually caused us more problems. I paid my sous chef a good wage because he was a strong person. If you've got one person there day in, day out, you know he'll pull everybody together and make it work, good staff or bad. We were fortunate because we employed two chefs on not a very good wage at all, but they wanted to get into catering. The idea was if they worked for me for a certain amount of time, they'd get paid so much, but they'd learn – get paid for learning, do the job at the same time – and at the end of it they'd get better jobs.

So you've got everything planned out, you know what you have to do. You've only got so much to spend, so you must cost out everything that you write down. You've only got a certain number of staff, a certain amount of space to cook the food in and plate it. You need to set your cooking standards to match the restaurant. No point in setting too high a standard at a place where it won't be appreciated. They don't want flash, fancy food. So you cook to a certain level and that's easy. The hardest part is getting everybody behind you, to work with you. That's where your own experience comes in. You need to make sure that each person is doing the job you want them to do. The way our kitchen was built you were facing the restaurant when you were cooking, but you needed eyes in the back of your head to see what was going on. You've got to do your job and keep an eye on everyone else. But gradually, if you're good enough, you can show the staff what they should be doing. Then when you're busy, you're cooking the food, confident that the person behind you is doing his job properly.

When you're starting up somewhere new, one of the basics is to set up with suppliers. This is nothing to do with the bosses now. They've laid down the budget, but that's as far as they go. I'm the chef, it's up to me to source my own supplies, set everything up, get the company stamp sent off to them, assure them we can pay within twenty-eight to thirty days. Restaurants come and go quickly, suppliers want their money on time. All in all, I had three meat suppliers down to see me. They came with bits of meat, with information, their price lists, delivery times. One came from Gillingham, one from west London, one from south London, all at different times. They then tried to sell their product at the best price. In the end I picked one out of the three. I was looking for the best prices, best guarantees of delivery, whether I could trust them to give me what I wanted. Usually I choose two, the second one to fall back on if there's problems with the first. Then I go looking for a veg supplier, in this case I used ones I'd known from Odette's onwards. When I went to Quag's I was dealing with suppliers I already knew. So you bring in three, decide on two (one of them as a back-up). Then it's the dry-goods suppliers.

So you've decided on your suppliers, decided on the menu, you know how much you're going to sell it for, know how much profit you're going to make, then you've got to decide what part of the kitchen it's going to come from. You can't put hot soup in a cold larder if there's nowhere to keep the soup hot. You've got to put stockpots on very first thing in the morning; you've got to get your sauces cooking first thing in the morning too – that's all thought out. All that has to be prepared, so that come twelve o'clock, the start of the service, all the prep will have been done, in the fridges, ready to go and now you're ready to start cooking the food. So you have to plan which part of the kitchen it's going to come from.

The cold starters will come from the cold larder. The cold starter chef is usually someone who's just training, getting used to working with food. Slicing, washing salads and so on. Then you've got your sauce section. Your meat and fish all come from one section. Then you've got a grill behind you, so you think, 'The grill chef can do the grills and fries, he can warm up the hot soup, he can warm up the veg that goes as a side dish.' At the SBC, one person would do the sauce section and run the pass – he's calling the checks out to the people behind him as well as cooking the food. When the checks come in from the waiters he calls out the dishes to his brigade, who get on with the cooking. This ensures that they always have a dish ready for when it will be wanted. When he wants to send the food to the restaurant he shouts for what he wants – all the orders for a given table – and the other chefs bring the dishes up to the pass where they're plated and then sent over the pass to a waiter.

What you have to realise, if you've put ten grilled dishes on, and one pan-fried fish dish with a sauce, everything's going to be coming from the grill and the person on the sauce is going to have nothing to do. So when you write your menu you have to think, 'Let me make sure I've got three or four dishes that he can be doing, and I'll be doing five or six of the other dishes. I can cook mine a bit quicker than the grill would, and then I'm ready to go when he's ready to go. That's how you work it out. You couldn't have nine dishes coming from the sauce section and one from the grill section – that leaves the grill chef with nothing to do. You've got to level it out, work out how you're going to cook the food and where it's coming from, and while that's going on the larder section can get on with the cold starters.

At somewhere like Gleneagles, it's even easier. One chef would write a menu, say, and the soldier ants would do it for him. He'd write a menu for each of the different outlets – Gleneagles had five different restaurants. He'd take that menu to the head of each restaurant, and the head chef running that part would say to the people under him, 'This is what we're going to do.' At Gleneagles, there were three commis chefs on the larder, four chefs on the sauce, four on the grill in the main restaurant. The chefs at a place like Gleneagles are probably more skilled than other chefs. If you go to a Harvester at lunchtime, they're going to do a hundred covers too. The difference is that a lot of their food is ready-cooked. So the Gleneagles chef might write out a big menu, but he's got so many chefs to carry it out. Whereas for me, if I've got a new boy on the larder behind me, and I've got to show him his job while doing mine, that's different. If you have five chefs on one section you don't have to worry about that. And there are more hands to cut and prepare the food, plate it and get it up.

When I'd found my suppliers, written my menu, the next thing was to write out my recipes – all the ingredients, their weights, the method of cooking the dishes, the prices and thus the cost of every dish. When you've decided what dishes you'll use, you then have to work out what the gross profit will be on each one. Your costing sheet tells you that. You know you're going to use an 8 oz sirloin steak, costing say £2.10 to serve. If I put this salad on and sell it for £4, am I going to be making my 72 per cent from it? You need to make an average of

70 per cent on everything you do. Some dishes you'll make 90 per cent on, but some only 65 per cent.

So you weigh out the ingredients for every dish and cost them all out, working on the basis of each individual dish. You can make a tart, and you know you'll be getting ten slices out of it. So you divide the cost of the whole tart by ten, which gives the individual cost price per portion. This allows you to work out the selling price. You follow the same principle whatever the dish. If I'm going to do a batch of lamb shanks – it's best to do about forty at a time – the best way is to make the whole lot first. And, in the same way as with the tart, you divide the whole dish by the number of portions you want to get out of it. Once again that gives you the cost price and lets you calculate the selling price. So you start off with forty portions of this, forty portions of that, but break it down to the cost of one portion. You might get it down to £1.50 a portion. So you think: £1.50 a portion, it's a main course, not bad, not costing a lot, but what am I going to make on it? So you work out what you're going to sell it at, plus VAT, and I always put 5 per cent wastage on every dish I make. I don't have to think about waiters' wages, that's a separate budget. My budget is for my food. Just food costs. That's what I'm working on.

So I've got a lamb shank that cost me £1.50 per portion. But on top of that I have to take into consideration the garnish. I've got a Roquefort *dauphinoise* to go with it, costed independently. I've got three separate costing sheets for my shank, my *dauphinoise*, my sauce, and then one more sheet for the actual dish itself. Now I've made up my forty lamb shanks, I've costed it all out, I've taken the price of one portion out of that forty on to a new sheet, and on the next sheet I've got the costing of one tray of dauphinoise; I've taken one portion out of that one tray and put it on to my sheet with my lamb shank, and then I'll put 2p maybe for a sprig of watercress. I've also done a costing sheet for the sauce, however many litres, and taking so many millilitres out to go on the single plate. Then I add all that up and that's my cost per dish.

Once I've worked out the costing sheet it tells me how much I should sell this dish at to make a 70 per cent profit, which is the average profit margin that top restaurants use. This costing system, which was developed by a chap with a west London restaurant, lets you calculate a 70 per cent profit in four simple steps and will also tell you how much your profit will be from the actual selling price of your dish. So it tells me how much I need to make a 70 per cent profit, but also tells me how much I'm selling it at. Or rather, it tells me what profit there is on the price I've decided on. But the truth is, if I really sold everything to make no more than 70 per cent as the system told me, then I'd lose. You don't make any profit on things like vegetable oil and dry goods, miscellaneous bits and pieces like tomato paste, salt and pepper, butters, creams. So when you're costing a dish, you're not just looking for a profit on the dish itself, but to cover everything else as well. So if I make 83 per cent profit, that extra 13 per cent pays for all the dry goods, the miscellaneous items.

We had no costing sheets at Odette's. I was sous chef and there were about five of us in the kitchen. So we ordered our food, and if we were told the food cost was too high, we'd look at the dishes we were doing and then decide either to do another dish, use a different cut of meat, or simply charge a bit more for what we were doing already. If I wasn't working for a company, I could do the menu day in and day out without bothering with costing sheets. If I owned my own restaurant, with a couple of chefs in the kitchen, because I've got costing knowledge, I wouldn't need costing sheets. But at SBC I was responsible to a company, and that's the same now. Every group that owns restaurants, they want proper accounting in each one. And it does give you extra confidence, once you've done your costings, knowing you're all right, you've costed everything out to make more than 70 per cent profit. And the managers can take those sheets to the directors and show them how that kitchen is doing.

In the end, sadly, SBC didn't work. The real problem wasn't the size of the kitchen, or the hard work we had to put in. It was the company policy. The way I saw it, SBC was about selling beer, and the food, however good we tried to make it, came second. The food was meant to be bringing people in to drink more beer. But it didn't work. Lunchtime failed: the menu was too heavy. So we changed the lunch menu to a lighter one. We took off the *à la carte* and put on sandwiches, scrambled eggs, sausage and mash, and so on. Then it started to take off. But eventually the original owners, who realised that it wasn't going to make them the kind of money they expected, sold it on to another entrepreneur. The new owner wanted big changes in the food concept. I stood my ground, saying, 'No, we don't want to be doing chips in the bar, sandwiches at night time in the middle of serving *à la carte* food.' In the event I didn't stay much longer, a better opportunity came along. Once I had moved on, they got their own way, but it just didn't work out. The idea was good food, good beer, lots of profit, happy people. But while it was good food and good beer, it was still losing money. That was it.

CHAPTER EIGHT

SUPPLIERS

Every morning, before most offices open, Soho has its own special rush hour: the pilgrimage of the white vans. They tour the area's restaurants, bringing with them the supplies that make the food business possible. From the major markets – New Covent Garden for fruit, veg and flowers, Smithfield for meat and Billingsgate for fish – or from individual suppliers who in turn may have been to the big markets, but are equally likely to have arranged their own sources of supply, both from the UK and, especially in the case of meat, abroad. Choosing the right supplier, from the many who compete for his order, is one of the head chef's basic skills. It may not be necessary, or within the budget even possible, to fly in vegetables from Rungis (Paris's version of Covent Garden, and like it exiled from the centre to the periphery – Les Halles, like the old Covent Garden is now one more homogenised tourist attraction) but the purchase and preparation of the best possible ingredients has to be fundamental to top-level cooking.

Learning to deal with suppliers is one of the things the head chef has to do. Research them, check them out and order from them.

Nowadays, there's lots of suppliers and they want your business badly, so you can pick and choose. The capital's filling up with new food outlets every day, and the more restaurants that open the more business there is for the suppliers, and the more business they've got, given the competition, the better they have to be. It's obviously easier for a supplier to look after a kitchen that's taking £15,000 worth of goods a week from him than a kitchen that's only taking £1,500. But what makes what I'd call a 'quality' supplier is that, whether you're the big kitchen or the small one, they provide you with exactly the same quality of food and service. It makes sense. After all, some of the chefs in the small kitchens might one day move to a big kitchen and when they get there they might want to get rid of the suppliers who they find. So if they've had that quality supplier in their small kitchen, the first thing they'll do is ring him up and give him their business, knowing that he looked after them well before.

When I agree to use a supplier I give him the specifications, say, for the fish: fillet this, slice that, give me such and such a weight of salmon per side, that sort of thing. That's what I want and that's the way I want it prepared. I don't want anything different. Those specs are based on the menus I've written and the dishes we cook. So the fish supplier will tell me, 'Yes, we'll supply you with so and so,' but if he doesn't meet the agreed specification he can have it all back and I'll buy it off someone else. Say he sends me my sea bass and it comes in whole – not filleted or pinboned (the removal of very fine bones) or scaled, when I asked for it to be done like that – back it'll go.

Suppliers are very competitive. They all promise to give you best produce at the best price. Suppliers who are after your custom will always try to undercut your regular guys, but though a supplier might knock 5 per cent off now, he'll add it on to something else later. So I think, 'No, if I want to use you, I will. But just offering it cheap isn't going to tempt me.' A lot of my suppliers are more expensive than others in the group, but I get better quality, plus I use it well. That means I can still make a better profit. If I used some of those second-rate suppliers I'd make even more profit, but what's the point? Yes, it costs less, but the quality won't be as good. So whether it's cheap or expensive, the bottom line is still how you use it. Of course, like every other chef I have a budget, so I can't just buy where I like. For instance, I can't use an organic chicken – knowing what I have to make in profit, I just can't afford it. And there's no point in going to an expensive supplier, however fantastic he is, if it cuts into your gross profits. It isn't that you can't afford everything he's selling, just not some of the items. I can't afford to buy truffles, at £140-odd a kilo. The budget won't stretch that far.

Of course there's plenty of scope for corruption. And believe me, there are cowboys out there who'll sell whatever garbage they can get away with. There was a classic example at 'a well-known London restaurant'. Now in a big restaurant or a hotel either the chef will do the ordering, ringing it all through himself, or he'll get the goods receiver to do it. The goods receiver collects the food at the back door, checks it, weighs it, checks the quality, puts it in the right fridge in the right place – old produce at the top, new at the bottom, the usual way it's done. The food purchaser, next one up from the goods receiver, checks the prices, does the food invoices and the rest of the paperwork, and checks with suppliers what the price will be next day. The chef himself won't be dealing with the company direct. The goods receiver gets that information from the purchaser and will then tell the chef the prices. He then thinks, 'Right, I'll order the fish from him and him, and if he brings his prices down tomorrow, I'll order from him.' So there was this goods receiver at this 'West London restaurant' who was ringing suppliers up and saying, 'You need to give me backhanders. If you don't, I'll tell the chef your prices are higher.' Faced with that the supplier panics – the last thing he wants is to lose this major account – comes to an agreement and offers a back-hander. The receiver got away with it for a while, but the management found out what was going on because eventually one of the suppliers got fed up with being blackmailed and rang up the chef and told him what was happening. The restaurant brought in an undercover agent, a private eye, and he was given a full-time job as a goods receiver. He didn't look like a goods receiver and people eventually realised why he'd been employed. But everyone kept quiet and let the goods receiver go on for another three months while the undercover guy gathered all the evidence. And after that he was arrested.

In a smaller place it would have to be the chef who ran the scams. You'd say something like, 'I'm giving you £60,000 worth of business a year, you need to do something for me.' You'll have perhaps a meat, fish or veg supplier who's struggling to get business, and they will pay off a chef to get that business. The chef could think, 'I can double my salary just by buying my meat off this guy. If his meat's not good enough, I'll still use it, obviously, to keep my money.' But most chefs know all the suppliers and have known them for years, so it doesn't happen a lot. It's not really worth it: either professionally or even as far as the money goes. But it *does* happen – of course it does.

There's a meat supplier I know who was providing cheap sirloins and fillets and everybody was using him. Now, when you buy a sirloin, you should also get the fillet attached to that sirloin. If you buy 'a sirloin', he bones it, portions it and sends you the fillet and trimmings from it, as part of the price. What he was doing was keeping the fillet back. He was just sending the sirloin. And then selling you the fillet separately, cheaper than everybody else. And people didn't notice, they were just pleased the sirloin was so cheap. But I noticed straight away when I started using him. You expect to pay about £9 a kilo for a sirloin, £12 a kilo for fillet. But he was charging maybe 20 per cent less. I changed from him to someone else.

Fish suppliers can sell you what is supposed to be fresh fish, which is in fact frozen, defrosted fish. There's about £2 a kilo difference in price between frozen and fresh. That's about all a fishmonger can do. The fish suppliers are quite good.

Fruit and veg suppliers have more scope than the others. But if they send you rubbish, you just send it back; they're out the window and you use somebody else.

As for actually stealing the food after it's arrived in the kitchen, there isn't much of that really. You're working with it all day and at the end you just want to go home. I can take things home — the butcher usually sends it for free anyway. But there's not much nicking, and those that do it always get found out. At Odette's, being small, everyone knew what was going on, so you couldn't do it. At Quag's, none of the staff ever nicked. Sometimes the sous chef would say, 'Would you mind if I take that home?' That was it. The KPs just nick it from the pigswill bin. Or they'll pick at food off a plate that's just come back from a table: that's totally mad — who knows if the customer's got HIV or anything?

Ordering the right quantity of food comes down to good food management. Experience. When I first started at Soho Soho I thought the previous chef had been ordering too much, which first of all made the fridges look untidy — you just had to look at them to know that you've got too much food. It's a judgement call to ensure you have just the right amount of food to go on the table. You've also got to have the right fridges to put it in, and even if you've got brand-new fridges, the contents has to be carefully controlled by the chef.

So to get your food ordering right, you've got to have the right place to put it in. We've got two restaurants here, which does give a bit of back-up: so if you walk into a *mise en place* fridge upstairs at seven p.m. and there's no steak sitting in front of you, but you know you've got fifty in the service fridge downstairs, you're fine. I know what's in our fridges, what I'm going to use per day. We have ordering sheets and all the produce we use, on the basis of what we need for the current menu, is written down. I go through my fridges every night to do my ordering. If I've got a full tray of oranges, I know I won't use a full tray the next day, so they're not ordered. I need to know I've got full trays of oranges, or aubergines or peppers – we use a lot of those – and if we've got two trays in on a Friday for Saturday, I'll be fine. So if I make sure those trays are full every day I know I'm going to be OK.

On a Monday night you never expect to run out of food, never never never. Monday to Thursday you should never run out of food. On Friday and Saturday you might get caught out now and again, but you try to make sure you've got a menu with good quality and a good range, in both fish and meat, and that should keep you covered. Of course some things are more popular – you always have to have steak on the menu, and you get fed up serving steak – but you make sure you have plenty in stock. Because we've got such quality fridges, I know if I order a Scotch sirloin it's going to be good until – well, the longer the better really. There's the odd time we'll run out of steak around ten-thirty p.m. upstairs. But we never run out at nine.

I'd like to think that we could sell a bit of everything on the menu. I'll make sure that I have at least a dozen portions of each dish in the fridge. I shouldn't be selling all my Scotch beef or my sea bass, because I've written a menu with dishes to appeal to every sort of person. If I couldn't write a menu to appeal to everybody I'd just put 'Scotch beef' and that'd be it. I try to write a menu that everybody will like. In the first week of the new menu I always make sure I've got plenty of everything because I don't know what's going to sell. But after the second week I get an idea. We get a print-out of what we've sold the most of. We're selling a good mix of everything at the moment, which is a good sign.

But the fridges are going to hold out. The fish is going to hold out from Tuesday to Thursday. If we've still got it on Friday and it smells good, I'm not going to bin it. It's down to me to smell the food, to taste it. If I can taste one piece of cod out of six and it tastes good, well I'll serve the rest. If I bin it all I've lost out on everything. That's my fault. Meat is pretty simple, but fish is quite difficult. On Tuesday you can get good fish, on Monday not really. You have the fish you're going to use that day in the fridge, but you've got back-up for the next day. So starting from Tuesday I get two lots of fish in. I can get twenty portions of sea bass in on a Tuesday and know I won't even use ten. Then I use ten and buy another ten on Wednesday, but use Tuesday's on Wednesday, and Wednesday's on Thursday. If you're a busy fish restaurant, you don't have the problem. You can over-order a little bit knowing you can sell it at lunchtime the next day. You're ordering enough to do that day's dinner and the next lunch. When it comes to Saturday, you look at the bookings on Friday night, see what's in the fridge and think, 'Just get a few more portions of this.'

The only food we'll run out of is the Special of the Day. And that's OK. It's a one-off dish for the day and if it sells well we've done well. Sometimes it's true that the Special isn't special, it can be anything you need to use up. You might have too much sea bass in and not sell it on the Tuesday and Wednesday, so on Thursday you put it on Special, sell it cheaper, do it simply, with a simple garnish. Say we do a party for eighty, they pay for eighty people, but twenty don't turn up. Lucky us, we can use that food to sell in the restaurant: that unsold party food becomes the Special.

Ordering for a restaurant is very different from the way you do it in a hotel. In a hotel they have their goods receiver, a goods manager, and you'd just end up with the meat or whatever you needed just being brought up to be cooked. In a small restaurant it's all there in front of you. You order the food yourself, you do everything yourself, you check the food, you prep it, cut it, cook it — you do everything. In a hotel you don't see that. And the hotels are chains. When I worked at the Mercury it got turned into a Ladbroke hotel. Everything delivered had Ladbroke labels on it, already prepped. And any Ladbroke hotel had exactly the same food. In a restaurant you order for that day, run out, get fresh in the next morning and just keep going. You don't have big freezers. You've got one big walk-in fridge, then your section fridges. And you buy fresh every day.

Before the vans can make their way to Soho, they must be filled. And if restaurant kitchens are working from seven in the morning to past midnight, then the suppliers who provide their raw ingredients fill in what's left of the day. All night and every night suppliers of fruit and vegetables, fish and meat, are working away. At Smithfield, London's meat market for more than half a millennium (although the live cattle and poultry haven't been driven through the City streets since 1868, when that part of the market was resited at the Caledonian Market in north Islington), the juggernauts start pulling in around nine p.m., and by midnight they've backed up to the unloading bays, great processions of dangling carcasses making their way to the wholesalers' butcheries and stalls. Andrew has opted out of Smithfield. Like many restaurants he prefers a smaller supplier, in his case British Premium Meats, which is out on a bleak industrial estate in Wembley. Here rooms full of butchers tackle beef, lamb, pork and hundreds of chickens and ducks every night: cutting them up and preparing them to the exact specifications demanded by London's chefs. The storeroom fills with cardboard boxes, each one named. The boxes move to the vans and thence into the early-morning streets.

We had two butchers when I joined Soho Soho and I knew one of them was lousy. So I dropped him. I wasn't guaranteed quality every day and he'd just say, 'We-e-ell . . . can't get any more of that this week.' I'd say, 'You're a butcher, you *can* get it.' Didn't make any difference. He went. Now we get ours from British Premium Meats, out in Wembley. They're very good. They employ seventy-five staff, including drivers for their twenty-two vans, delivering to around 450 outlets all over London. It's a twenty-four-hour day operation, a business that could turn over at least £10 million a year in sales. Not bad for brothers who started out with a small shop and one van. The skilled areas in the butchery are filled with butchers preparing meat constantly. One bloke slices Parma ham all day. There's a place where they do all the offal, another where they do the game, another for poultry, all different rooms. We have our own shelves there. Ordering is obviously tied in with what I've got on the menu. I get the butcher in, I need to find out how much 180-gram veal portions will cost. Scotch fillets, lamb shanks. I want to know the cost for each. Black-leg chickens – can he get them for me? *Boeuf bourguignonne* – what type of beef can we have for

that? Staff foods – I have to feed the staff, chefs and front of
house, as well, so what can he provide for them? When I'm
writing a menu for the private dining room, I have to find out if
he can provide the cuts I want for it, and if he will be able to get
them all the time. I need to make sure he faxes me over the price
list every day.

The suppliers all have to have these health and safety certificates. Our butcher has top marks in all the hygiene certificates
and is very proud of that. Even so, you do sometimes get 'off'
meat. When you take on a new butcher, when he sends you your
first week's goods, you're impressed, think he's all right, then it
starts dipping down, the meat's a bit dodgy. I sent some back the
other week because it stank. A sirloin that had been cut for me.
But I smelt the bones and they stank. The butcher apologised and
rectified it immediately. His attitude was, 'If I've given you one
bad thing, you can have two good things to make up.' We don't
have a lot of bad meat any more.

Like Smithfield, Billingsgate, London's oldest fish market, has been
abandoned by many restaurants. Andrew uses a supplier called Daily
Fish, sited on another industrial estate, this one in the grimy wastelands
north of King's Cross. Again it's an all-night job. Big trucks arriving early
– a whole juggernaut filled with salmon – small ones, owned by Daily
Fish, setting off into the dawn. And all through the night a row of
experts making their way through eight hours' worth of fish orders,
grabbing the fish – five dozen scallops, half a giant tuna, ten sides of
salmon – and, like the butchers, cutting, slicing and filleting to the
specifications posted for each individual restaurant. And again there
are the cardboard boxes, piled in their dozens, each labelled for the
restaurant for which the fish is destined.

With fish you rarely get anything bad, it's just either too big or too small. Our main fish supplier gets a lot of it straight up from the south coast: Cornwall, Devon, wherever. Salmon, scallops, crayfish from Scotland, langoustines. Lobsters from Dorset. But we don't do a lot of seafood. Our fish supplier is one of the very best and the volumes they handle are amazing: they buy and sell up to 2 tons of sea bass each week, 500 kilos of live crabs, 5.5 tons of salmon, 400 kilos of live scallops, 250 kilos of live lobsters, 400 kilos of smoked salmon, a ton of mussels, 1,000 oysters, 150–200 kilos of live langoustines, plus prawns and fish especially prepared for fish-soup mixes. He's got nineteen vans, fifty-six staff and an annual turnover of at least £12 million. (Three or four years ago he was bringing in £4–5 million.) Again this is a twenty-four-hour operation with plenty of fish preparation specialists working with ice-cold fish in very cold temperatures through the night.

There's only a few bigger fish suppliers: some of those might be twice as big, but the quality certainly isn't twice as good. Years ago everyone bought their fish from Billingsgate; these days at Billingsgate you have to wait till three or sometimes five a.m. for stuff to be unpacked. So the main suppliers deal directly with the suppliers on the coast. The only time Daily Fish use Billingsgate is when they can't find what you want elsewhere – or when they've run out of what they've had delivered already. (Same thing goes for the butchers: the days of getting everything from Smithfield are over. They prefer to do it direct, whether from the UK or, for instance with buckets of veal, from Holland, or some of the poultry from France. It's all about quality.) So I'll give my supplier a spec, he'll give that spec to his supplier. He might get a six-kilo wild salmon off one supplier in the season, and the rest of the time he uses another supplier who'll give him four-kilo farmed salmon. We use farmed salmon. Wild salmon is only good in the summer. With farmed salmon, it's got a bashed-up nose, the tail's crooked, and the flesh is deep red because of the pellets they're fed. The wild salmon are nice and pink, no bashed-up noses and no tails bashed up either. The reason that farmed salmon are bashed up is that they are reared in thousands, all packed together in a small area of water. You don't get that problem with the wild fish. Farming's used more and more, but the truth is that, though you can always get it, the quality's not the same. All these fish, salmon, turbot, halibut, get fed the same stuff, which means they all end up tasting similar. Which is a pity, but in the end you're back looking at your budget, and wild fish is very, very expensive.

Like Billingsgate, now resited far from its origins on Upper Thames Street out near Canary Wharf on the Isle of Dogs, Covent Garden, which was once at the very heart of the metropolis, hasn't actually been in Covent Garden since 1974. Once the kitchen garden of Westminster Abbey, the area became a full-scale market in 1670 as shops and stalls grew up around the piazza erected by the Duke of Bedford forty years earlier. Now in purpose-built buildings at Nine Elms in Battersea (itself for many years a major Thames-side trading wharf) it remains the most important wholesaler of fruit, vegetables and flowers in the country. Today's market falls into two, possibly three parts. A central core contains the major wholesalers, selling to everyone, in and out of London and indeed in and out of the UK. Sited in a circle around this central market are the specialist wholesalers who provide restaurants with their supplies. It is from one of these, Chef's Connection, that Soho Soho gets the bulk of its fruit and vegetables. There is a third side to the Garden, stuck away under the railway arches that run alongside the main market. Here, people work through the night to peel and pack potatoes, carrots and any other vegetable that chefs need prepared.

Fruit and veg come from New Covent Garden, at Nine Elms in London. They get deliveries from all over the country. Huge vans will appear and serve twenty wholesalers with potatoes, for example. Then the strawberry people arrive, the cauliflower people, the mushroom suppliers, and so on. And a lot comes from abroad. There's one big supplier in the market who bought his own truck about five years ago, huge thing, and he sends it to France every Monday morning, comes back Tuesday night, bringing back really nice stuff. You've got single suppliers in Covent Garden who just do mushrooms, say, and they get them from everywhere. Some do just French produce or Italian; as well as Nine Elms you've also got the wholesale side of Spitalfields market in the East End, which concentrates on ethnic stuff – spices, exotic fruits and veg, and so on. But Covent Garden is the main one. Obviously they deal mainly with London, although they send stuff all over the country; sometimes even outside – which means you get the situation where a country exports stuff to London and then buys it back from Nine Elms – but mainly it stays at home. Back in Ellesmere Port our suppliers would get their stock from Liverpool. You'd get potatoes from Shropshire, Yorkshire. Gleneagles would get their stuff from Glasgow. And I think there's a market in Birmingham. There must be markets in the main towns.

We get most of our veg from Chef's Connection, which supplies all sorts of top restaurants. I've used them now for over a year and with my fishmonger and butcher they're definitely what I'd call the quality suppliers. As a chef you need to trust your suppliers and I trust them. Each month they send out a market report, which helps me decide on the sort of stuff we'll be cooking. It's quite detailed, explaining not just what's about, but what's coming up, and whether things are good, or not so good. You'll get something like, 'POTATOES: Graded large Desirée, good for chipping, boiling and baking. Maris Piper, good for chipping, roasting, baking and mashing. Cyprus Diamonds were the best for chipping, but have now finished. Cyprus Spunta now replace them, probably the best all-purpose potato. Fir Apple potatoes available, good for salads, as are Truffle potatoes – dark skin mauve flesh, also good for salads. Ratte potato excellent salad potato. Large graded King Edwards. Italian large Spunta, also very good. Be warned, all large potatoes going up in price.' Or 'TOMATOES: A few varieties of plum tomatoes available. Salad tomatoes from Spain have improved. Tomatoes on vine very good, as are cherry tomatoes on vine. Baby plum tomatoes are available but not always guaranteed. Dutch green, yellow and orange tomatoes are finished. Yellow cherry tomatoes are available. Salad tomatoes, Single M and Double M, which are the normal size salad tomatoes, are not as sweet as the smaller MMM, which are beautiful. If you just order tomatoes we will give you the normal MM.' All very helpful and every supplier's doing the same thing for its customers.

They have eight to ten vans, twenty-six staff, and about two hundred customers and probably a turnover of about £5–6 million which is good for a supplier in the fruit and veg trade who's dealing with quality rather than quantity. Bigger suppliers may make more money, but they don't provide the quality of produce and individual service that Chef's Connection does. Every day their main buyer is going round the market, ordering for the next day. At Covent Garden you've got two markets in one: one in the middle that all the veg suppliers to the trade are buying off; then there's this outer rim, with people like Chef's Connection, buying from the main wholesalers on the basis of the orders they get from their restaurants. In a way they're like vegetable shops, only they do the sorting out and the choosing, and stick it all in bags and baskets on pallets out the front. However, the ingredients they get you are much superior to the average greengrocer's or supermarket. The way it goes is I'll ring up their main buyer, tell him what I need, and he'll say, 'I'll get this for you tomorrow.' Then he goes into the middle of the market to the wholesalers and buys off them. Obviously they get used to what a certain chef is ordering and what we've ordered for Tuesday was probably bought on Monday on the assumption we'd need it. I ring through my order no later than eleven-thirty at night. When they get it it's placed on their computer, printed out. They have all the different restaurants ordering, so they look at the print-outs and one driver will have, say, twenty restaurants to deliver to. So when he comes in in the morning, around three or four o'clock, he'll be loading up his van, picking up the orders that have been prepared for each restaurant — which have already been checked for quality and weight. Then they move them to the van, checking them again as they go on. They'll have to run round to get things they haven't got in stock. While that's going on, the buyer's back going round the market looking to buy everything for the next day. His main job is to search for quality and there's only a select few wholesalers who reach that quality.

So by the time the ingredients arrive on the table you've got the wholesaler's price, my supplier puts his price on top, then I put mine on top of that. I pay about sixty pence for a kilo of new potatoes. At a supermarket you probably pay £2 for a kilo. There's one big supplier in the market who supplies, say, all the packed salads, or all the potatoes, for Sainsbury's in the London area. A lot of the suppliers have staff employed just to deal with one big restaurant group. Say the group wants a stir-fry veg mix. The supplier will sell it for maybe £2 a kilo, and he'll have to employ someone to cut it all up and make up every box the same. So in every ten kilo box there'll be twenty peppers, twenty onions, and so on, all ready.

A lot of prep is done at Covent Garden these days: you can get peeled potatoes, turned carrots cut into different shapes — there's a lot of prep they do. Turned carrots are done in a barrel shape, or they'll cut them into strips. I always get my potatoes peeled there. I can ring the veg man and say; 'I need 20 kilos of peeled large potatoes,' and they do it. That saves your staff peeling potatoes all day, but that also means that the work will be done mainly by cheap labour who don't have any real interest in the job. Because of that I don't get much done for me, only the potatoes, and chips.

I do our meat and fish prep myself. Checking it out, cutting, slicing, marinading the things that need marinading, slicing up the salmon ready for cooking, making sure every piece is the same weight, that sort of thing. Then putting it away in the fridges. On a Monday, which is when the biggest orders come in, you're dealing with around £1,000 worth of meat and fish. The vans arrive sometime between eight and nine and it takes me two and a half to three hours to get it all prepared.

But I leave the more basic prep to the suppliers. I'm not cleaning fish or chickens, tackling great sides of beef. You're so busy, you don't have the time. The suppliers want your business so they'll do everything for you — if it's fish, they'll scale it, pinbone it, and so on. If you need twenty salmon for a big party the next day, the fishmonger just says, 'Don't worry about it, I'll cut it up in portions.' And he doesn't charge for doing that – he wants to keep your business. Apart from saving time, it saves money: I can save the wages I'd have to pay a prep chef. Getting this level of prep done before you have the food delivered means that work in the kitchen is a lot easier nowadays. A lot of places don't employ butchers any more – the prep gets done for them by the supplier. So it's easier for the kitchens, but harder for the butcher. Because of the amount of competition, a butcher has to prep the meat, trim the steaks, cut the fillets, clean up and slice the calves' liver. Anything you need doing can be done by the supplier now. And of course you get to rely on it: if you rang your butcher with an order and he said, 'Oh, you'll have to butcher it and cut the portions yourself,' you'd be horrified. Yet all that used to be done in-house. Even at Odette's, which is a small place, we did all that ourselves. We'd cut our own *entrecôtes* and so on. It wasn't until I worked at Quag's that basic foodstuffs came in prepped. It all depends on the chef, but very few can find the time any more and in a lot of kitchens there isn't the space for a prep chef. If you're ordering, say, twenty sides of salmon at one time, you need it already prepped. You could not physically cope with that in-house. Even at Quag's: it's big, but it's still a tight kitchen, there'd just be no room to do it. Michelin-starred kitchens are more likely to do all the prep themselves, but even they get some of their stuff prepped. Their supplier will know exactly what they want and he definitely won't mess up.

Of course the downside of all this is that it means if you're not doing it in-house those skills are dying among chefs. I was quite lucky to be able to learn it. I started to learn butchery at

Gleneagles, then did more at Billesley Manor. The Royal Lancaster had their own butcher, who did all the fish and meat prep in-house. Today you've got people working in these big restaurants, but they're not learning as they did years ago. When I go into a kitchen and I'm serving salmon, at least I know how to fillet it. If I have the time, I try to teach the boys, but often I don't have the time. Occasionally I make a point of buying in salmon unprepped to show them how to do it. What sort of fish is it? It's a pink fish. OK: then is it a flat fish, an oily fish, a round fish, how many fillets has it got? That kind of thing. There are good economic reasons for buying food in ready-prepped, but it's a great shame that the staff are not learning those skills any more. For me, it's still something worth knowing, and I think a good chef ought to find time to learn it. The problem now is that there are too many restaurants in London and chefs just don't have the time. Chefs who have studied well and know what they're doing are always going to be fine. But the commis chefs coming in now, OK they'll know how to run a big place, but where's the depth of experience, the basic knowledge about cuts of fish, cuts of meat, simple things like knowing that putting a lid on green vegetables turns them brown . . .?

CHAPTER NINE
M E N U S

The menu is the interface between kitchen and customer. It is, as it were, the chef's own market stall, where he lays out his wares, offering up his culinary skills for the buyer's delectation. And like many interfaces it's generally taken for granted. You look, read, ponder, choose, you may even ask the waiter what such-and-such a dish actually is, but rarely if ever does a customer wonder how and why the menu is as it is. Writing a menu is another basic but all-important skill. Far from being a wish list, it represents the coming together of a number of factors — kitchen equipment, the skills of the brigade, the promoted style of the restaurant, the budget for buying the ingredients and the pricing levels that the chef sees as correct. All these combine, as it were, to get the food on our plates.

When you make menus, you do think, 'Yes, this is food that should be nice to eat,' but on top of that you have to ask whether it's going to look nice. Is it really going to taste nice? You think about things and put them together in your head. You try it out and if it tastes good you say, 'OK, I'd eat it.' Because you'd never put anything on a menu if you yourself didn't like the taste. That said, you don't only go with stuff you like. For instance, I don't really like garlic, but other people do and for them we'll serve, say, a garlic mash with a lamb dish. I'll taste it, but I won't sit and eat a bowl of it. And if you turn that round, you can't do something that you like but other people don't. You want people to appreciate what you're doing and for you to appreciate that they like it. You want them to appreciate the whole dish in front of them. 'Can you tell the chef I really like that?' That's what you want to hear. You can't have them saying, 'I hate that,' and as the chef you're coming back with, 'Well *I* like it.' Anyway, there's ego, don't forget: I have to show off to the kitchen, to show off to the restaurant. I have to get it right.

The other thing you have to think of is the season. Although you can get pretty much anything you want, whatever the time of year, people tend to like certain things at certain seasons and that's something you have to bear in mind. Although you try to work out what's best and what you're going to sell, you can't make absolute guarantees. There's one dish on every menu I've written – it's always on the starters – and I'm asking, 'Will it sell?' It's always the vegetarian dish. The first menu change I did was of a beetroot and potato and horse-radish salad; I'd put it on, we cooked it, but it didn't sell a lot. So when we changed the menu next we got rid of it. But most of the main courses, meat and fish, have never been a gamble. You can say with confidence, 'Right, I've got five dishes on the menu, I've got a meat, a chicken, a lamb dish and offal (so, that's a couple of red dishes, a couple of white) – someone's always going to want that.' So, yes, meat sells, but at the same time you know your menu's crap if everyone starts eating beef. You can't go wrong with beef, but it's hardly challenging. It's so predictable. And from a cooking creativity point of view it's just not very adventurous for the kitchen staff, to sell beef. On another level there's a commercial consideration: the most expensive item for us to buy is beef. It costs the customer quite a lot, but I still make probably the least profit on beef out of everything I cook. I make more on liver than on beef, so I want to educate people to eat liver instead. So it's about money, of course, but it's also about trying to make people see there's more on offer. You try to serve beef so many different ways. But it's frustrating because the truth is that all they want is a piece of steak.

I had what I thought was a good idea. We had a grilled dish on the menu and when I wrote the new menu, I thought we'd put a beef dish on as grilled dish of the day. Every day we'd do a grilled dish of meat and just change the meat whenever we wanted. We started with rump of lamb, then got sick of that and changed to beef. Then we changed it to calves' liver. That sold really well. Then when I changed to the next menu I thought, 'Christmas coming up, goose getting fat, I don't want to be doing too many main courses.' We'd have loads of work and it'd be too much work for the kitchen. So I thought I'd put beef on, and put it on as grilled beef – grilled fillet of beef with traditional grill garnish. The punters loved it, but it's getting to the stage now where we're selling too much of it.

But the fact is, yes, if you've got any ambition and imagination, you do want to educate them, to get them to eat good food, not just go for the steak every time. The best way to do that is to have your own restaurant, thirty to forty covers, a good front-of-house team and a menu that explains the food, to show them they can eat good food simply. People can only be educated by the people serving them. I can write a menu and the staff can think, 'Oh, it all sounds really nice, but . . .' I think it's up to the restaurant manager or the staff to say to a customer, 'Have you tried this?' But you can't really educate the public unless you've got your own little place where you can treat them like they're family, or the most important guests you've ever had – that's the only way to get through to them. London is so full of people who just want to eat. We feed 130 people in the restaurant on a Saturday, when it is absolutely packed. I don't think in that situation the staff could talk someone out of beef and into kidneys with mustard mash. If people go out and want roast beef, that's what they'll have. If they decide to try fish that night, that's what they'll do. The best thing you can hope for is word of mouth: people who eat out a lot have to educate others to try somewhere different.

After all that you could say offering a new dish is a gamble, but I don't really think so. On my new menu there's a chicken dish. I was going to do it with capers and a butter sauce. Now the butter sauce wouldn't have worked on it properly. I couldn't do it on the meat if it's on the fish. So I kept the capers, but made a piquant Worcester sauce/sherry vinegar/capers/shallots/garlic/chilli sauce and put that with the chicken. I'd never done that before. But is that really a gamble? You think, 'People will always eat chicken, and pasta will go with it well.' Chicken's a bland meat. I was going to use organic chicken, but that would have cost £12 a small bird. I use a larger four-pound free-range bird and it costs £3 a bird. I use the plump breasts upstairs, sell the legs downstairs. Out of one £3 bird I'm going to get nearly £40 back, because I've used it right.

One way of checking how a new dish is going is to see what comes back with the waiters. When we launch a new menu I always ask the waiters to stop before they scrape the plates into the pigswill: it gives me a quick way of seeing what's worked and what hasn't. Obviously if there's different left overs on each plate, it's not much help, but if the same thing keeps getting rejected I can draw the obvious conclusion.

When chefs write their first menu, they base it on what they've done in the past. When that works, when they know they can price it properly, serve it properly, then they'll start doing their own thing. So the first menu gets written on experience. When you come to change that menu, and all the ones that follow it, there's a lot to think about. That's what you sit on a bus and think about. Sometimes you just change the way you put certain things together. We try it out on the Special, and if it works there, then we know we can price it and it will sell well, and so it goes on the main menu. But if I want to change a whole dish, to get rid of one and come up with something completely new, I go to the restaurant manager and say, 'Look, I want to take this off the menu, it's not successful.' Then I'm getting on with its replacement. On top of that there's always cost: at certain times of the year certain ingredients will be more expensive and that plays with your profits. When that's the case it's cheaper to change the dish completely.

Dishes are also flexible, whatever you write on the menu. If I don't think a dish works, I change it mid-menu. I can fine tune it. Say I write the menu as 'Beef, parsnips and honey', as long as it's got those ingredients, I can do it whatever way I like. We used parsnip matchsticks on the beef, then we decided to do it differently. Now we peel the parsnips, cut them into quarter lengths, caramelise them in honey and black peppercorns, and the top of the parsnip which we can't cut into lengths, we cut up to make a purée. So I've changed that now, in the middle of a menu. But the ingredients, the tastes people see on the menu and order, are still there.

And when you've worked out what you're going to cook, there's all sorts of administration. You need recipes written out and the menus; you have to write sheets for people in the kitchen, you need to work out daily prep sheets – descriptions of the food – so you need to work out when you write a menu exactly what's going to be in every fridge . . .

At Soho Soho there's a difference between the upstairs and downstairs menus. Upstairs is obviously fine dining. Downstairs we've got a Rôtisserie, people booking tables for two, tables for ten. They want to eat quickly, have bottled beer on the table, there's a piano playing at night, so the music's going, they're having a ball, having parties, they're all pissed and they don't want to be waiting round for the food. They want plenty of it without paying too much. They just want a good time. So we have the option of things off the rôtisserie, lots off the grill — which is why we have one chef who just does the grill. One does the chips, risottos and pastas to go with it. One person doing the larder. The food's not as pretty, but it's still good quality. And you have to employ the right chef to do that type of food. A career chef would work upstairs, someone who wants to go far. A chef who enjoys his job, who's not too interested in getting to the top, he'll work downstairs. The commis chefs might get paid the same downstairs as they do upstairs, but the ones working upstairs, they're going to go somewhere, they're going to earn more money in the future. But that's not to say that they all aren't equally respected for what they do.

When I'm writing a menu I have to think not just about the punters but the kitchen staff as well. The foundation of a menu is a good solid head chef who manages his kitchen properly. And after that it's the rest of the brigade. The boys coming through want to work in a good kitchen. It's a challenge to keep chefs and one of the best ways to do it is to write good menus and cook good food. If my menus are lousy, no one will work for me. With the menus, we just try things out. On my last menu change, I wrote the menu for upstairs. Downstairs I guided the sous chef into it and we wrote half each. And the next menu I asked him to write out for me the way he thought best. Now I'll say whether I like it or not and if I don't like it I'll say, 'What we'll do, we'll stick with the idea of this, but we'll add this meat instead of that meat.' In the upstairs kitchen I've written the three menus by myself, but the next one I'll get my sous chef to help me with it. I listen to people from all areas. They can come to me and say, 'Chef, can we do this?' and I can say, 'No, because . . .' and they'll say, 'All right, fine.' Another time they'll think, 'That's not fair, he doesn't want to put my food on the menu.' Most of them will get involved in planning a menu. It's nice to get everyone involved. Ultimately, though, it's my menu, I'm putting it on the plate and I know I want it like this, that's why I wrote it. So they have to realise that what's going on the plate is what the chef wants and not what they want. They should be thinking, 'I know how chef wants it, I want it like that as well and I'm going to make sure it's really really good.'

If the sous chef comes up with a dish, I take into account first whether I think it will work, and second, if it's nice. As a sous chef, you're there as back-up, to help the chef, keep him going. If I get stuck or lost with my menus and recipes and ideas, he's the one I fall back on. You say to your sous chef, what do you think? He wants to be a head chef one day, so he'll put his thinking cap on. And if you like his ideas, or something about them, you use them. Even the commis contributes. He might have seen something in another restaurant which I can try out and use if it works. I don't know everything and the more ideas and inspiration you get from others, whether lesser or better than you, doesn't matter. You've got it for free. If it's good, you should take it on board. If I don't think it's good for the restaurant I won't use it, or maybe I'll take the idea away and use it in a different restaurant, where it works, later in life.

* * *

You really do have to think about every item on the plate before serving it up. When you look at a plate, you don't want all odd shapes, different sizes, it should fit together well – not too much greenery, not too much white or red. When you put a dish together, you think of the taste first, then you put it on the table and think, 'Well, it looks a bit unexciting.' So you add something to it to make it more lively. On the venison dish we do, the venison is red to pink, the sausage is cut at an angle, where it's quite brown, and the sauce and cabbage are red and dark colours. Just put a sprig of chervil on top and that makes the difference. Looks great; but however good it looks, it's got to taste good too. Food might look unbelievable on a plate, but taste like nothing. So taste first, layout second. Obviously some people look with their eyes without using their taste buds and can only see pretty things on a plate; but pretty things can sometimes taste like garbage.

But however hard you try and however well you think you've planned it out, there are dishes that just don't work. Or if they work as a dish they still don't sell. As I said, for me it was a beetroot salad with new potatoes and horseradish. I don't know why it didn't work. Maybe people thought it was something you could get in a Harvester. But it was a lovely dish. It wasn't plated the way I wanted it, the owners had their own ideas about that. I wanted to fan the cooked beetroot around the plate, put the potatoes in the middle with the horseradish *crème fraîche* mixed into it, and the salad on the top, which I'd done previously and it had sold very well. But the owners wanted it plated their way. That was my first menu: 98 per cent of the dishes went well and looked good. But that one dish didn't work. So we'd prep five or six portions only. And when we came to the next full menu change, we dumped it.

* * *

Management don't interfere with the day-to-day running of the kitchen, but they do take an interest in the menus. When I arrived I obviously inherited a menu and I had to go with that for a while. Then I started doing it my way. The first thing I did was work out what I thought I wanted to do, and try out the dishes by myself. Then I sat down with the directors and gave them a description of every dish that would be on the menu and why it would be there, and they all sat round, going, 'Yeah, mmm.' And I'd say, 'The reason why I want to do this is because of this, because of that . . . we'll be able to charge so much . . . it'll be nice and fresh . . .' and so on. They go, 'Fine, yeah', and they really loved everything on the menu. Then they said, 'But can you do that for a hundred and twenty people on a busy night?' To which I could say, 'Definitely,' because that was one of the things I had to consider when I was writing the menu. You think about the flavour, how it will look, how much you need to have *en place*, how much you should have in your fridges, then you think, 'Can we do this for a certain number of people?' Whatever we have on the menu we're going to have to cook for that number of people anyway. Which I explained, and they liked that. The next stage was one Sunday when we got a director in, plus the food purchaser, the overall restaurant manager, the general manager and the senior manager at Soho Soho, and then I cooked everything – 'Here you are, all my new dishes.' All the chefs helped me on the day, we presented the dishes and they went through the whole menu. I think they wanted me to change one thing (the presentation of the beetroot salad). But I thought: one thing out of fifteen dishes . . . And they just loved everything. I gave them the prices, the cost of the food and whatever else they needed to know. So we launched that menu and it worked. So when it came to the next menu they just said, 'Go ahead, give us a list of what you're going to do, we'll approve it, say whether we like it, and then it'll be fine.' But this time I didn't have to cook for them. Now when I change my menus, they know I've got my head screwed on, that they'll like it. But that doesn't mean that if they really don't like something, or are not too sure about it, they won't be on the phone straight away: 'Why are you doing this, blah-blah-blah.'

They do check up on me, they're in quite a lot. I don't think they're there to spy on me, they just come in to eat and enjoy it. If there's something wrong they'll say, 'I liked it, but . . .' The bottom line is that they know what I'm doing, what sort of restaurant I'm running. They realise we're not a Michelin-star restaurant, we're not Gordon Ramsay, we're not the Gavroche. We're a good restaurant, we've got a good concept and we're cooking it right. I'd never get a Michelin star in a restaurant like this. Why not? First, the waiting-on team isn't big and sometimes it isn't good enough. Second, I've got the restaurant, the Rôtisserie and the private room. And for all that lot, ideally, you need a lot more staff than I have. On top of that – look at any of the Michelin-level chefs – I'd need to put in eighteen hours a day to get exactly what I want. As it is, I know where I am and what I want to do: I just want to have good food in the restaurant, people coming back again for another meal, and to get a full restaurant as many nights a week as we can. The management trust me now. They know what I'm doing and let me get on with it. But if something goes wrong – they're there. Whatever it is. They know if something's gone wrong. The way I look at it, I might be good today, I might not be tomorrow. Obviously I know what I've got to get ready for next Friday's party, stuff like that, but as far as the big picture is concerned, I take it one day at a time all the time.

* * *

As a chef you've got to keep up with the food trends, who's cooking what, what's popular. It cuts two ways: you don't want to miss out on the food people want because that's the food that sells, but you also don't want to be cooking the same food as everybody else. You're all starting off with the same ingredients, but once the raw materials get inside your kitchen you've got to do them differently from everybody else. Ten restaurants can use the same suppliers, but it's what you do with the food that counts. On my last menu I had chickpeas. And there was hummus and couscous. We've got couscous back on. People like it. Lamb shank is now in fashion. I had it on my first menu because I knew how to do it. OK, everybody was doing it, but if it sells you can't go wrong. It's not what you use, but how you use it. Ten restaurants can do lamb shanks, one will do it well, nine badly. When you're planning a menu you use a little bit of what's fashionable, but what's fashionable keeps changing. Somebody starts doing something one way and everyone catches on to it. It's chefs who don't know what they're doing that go slavishly with the fashion. But if you stick to what you know, you build your own profile.

When you've got your ingredients you can cook them in the English way, the Provençal way, the Italian way, or the Pacific Rim way. So you have the same ingredients, but can get something very different from them. It's good being brought up to do the English way first, then you can break away and add things to it. Fashions in food are really the fashion of where you are, the style of cooking your restaurant offers. At one stage everyone was sushi mad. It was all over the place, but that didn't last. Most restaurants shouldn't be serving it – it's not what they're about. We're a French Mediterranean restaurant. We're not going to be giving you sushi. Fashions are about an ingredient or a dish that becomes popular, but they're also about presentation, the way it looks. With *nouvelle cuisine* it was minimal portions, colourful plates. But you can't give out half a plate of food and charge £50. That was early to mid eighties. Pheasant with raspberry sauce. Terrible combinations. It was brave to serve it. But, then again, you could say the customers were pretty naïve to accept it. Everything was separated on the plate, the veg, the garnish, but there wasn't a lot of it, it just looked pretty. Probably three or four chefs plating up one dish. It might have tasted all right, but there was hardly enough to tell. It was like serving badly scraped plates.

The Pacific Rim has been popular for a while now. When I was at Quag's there was a little bit of that because the head chef had worked in Australia, where it all began. Pacific Rim has a touch of the Oriental. You can have white radish, courgette, chilli, peppers, coriander and you pickle them and serve them raw. A lot of Pacific Rim food is raw, sushi-style, very light, with lots of dressings. Now you can do an Oriental coleslaw, putting in red onions, really fine cabbage and carrots, cook it off quickly. The fish is more fresh fish, and there's more fish used than meat. The Australians don't get a lot of meat.

One of the big things at Quag's was tuna — rolled in wasabe, a hot green horseradish mustard, then covered in coriander and peppercorns. It was cut into chunks and served raw, with noodles and soy, sushi vinegar, and that was it. I don't think it's that appealing myself. And it's not a line of cooking I'd want to go into. But it is popular and some chefs are going out to Australia and coming back with this kind of cooking. They want to roast pumpkin and pawpaws. Then in another restaurant you'd be looking at a completely different style. At Odette's you'd do things like make pea soup out of pea pods, really good soup too.

You made fishcakes out of fish trimmings, which everyone does anyway. Because it was a small place, you had to use everything to get what you wanted. You rolled over your menus all the time. You wrote the menus daily — most of it was almost the same and you just chopped and changed when you wanted to. You had to think of loads of ideas of what you were going to do with food and how you were going to create it.

The fashion now is classic French, but to do it slightly differently. The thing that's happening now is that chefs are being asked to cook food that the customer wants. I want my fish grilled, a bit of salsa with it, bit of bread, stir-fried veg — that's all. OK, they're not coming into the kitchens and ordering like that, but that's definitely what people want: simplicity. They prefer that simplicity to places where there are specific menus, loads of garnishes. A lot of chefs are being driven to cook for the punters, by which I mean the boss'll walk in saying, 'There's a lot of people out there, they want simple food, cooked the way they want it. Stick to your own ideas, but don't get too pretentious. Cook what they want.' And that's what gets done.

The more places you work at, the more you learn. If I'm working at Quag's and they want the sauce made like so, and I'm a chef de partie, that's the way I make it. Then I go somewhere else and if the new place has another way of making it and it's a good way, then I'll do it that way. When you're in the kitchen you don't use cookbooks, it's word of mouth. You should always have a book and pen, so you can write down new ways of doing things. But outside the kitchen, when you're researching new dishes, you do go to cookbooks, look at pictures and think, 'Oh, I like that, I'll try it.' When I wrote the first menu at Soho Soho most of it was based on what I'd read in Elizabeth David about Provençal cooking, what they ate at that time, what goes well with what. With her it's not a case of reading a recipe. She'd say, 'At this time of year in France, they eat this with that.' Oh right, well, I'll put those things together, but in my own style.

It is not merely the size that differentiates the hotel kitchen from the restaurant. Of late, with a number of highly talented chefs forsaking the restaurants where they made their names for the potentially even more lucrative world of hotel catering, traditions are gradually changing, but until recently the cooking styles on offer were very different.

One of the things I've learned is what a difference there is between restaurant cooking and hotel cooking. A definite difference. In the first place, as a hotel chef you do so much more: breakfast, room service, lunch, bar snacks at lunch, evening service with room service as well. But the real difference is in the style of cooking, the menu you offer, the dishes you put on it.

Traditionally there's no Mediterranean influence in hotel food, it's more the classic French stuff. In 1992 when I went to Odette's in Primrose Hill, I went from hotel food, which I'd been cooking at the Royal Lancaster, to restaurant food. It was a total revolution. Everything changed. In a hotel you've got a lot of fish mousses, pâtés, terrines, the classic melon balls in a liqueur, the *entrecôtes* with classic garnishes. You could call it a more old-fashioned approach. The Dover soles are grilled whole, you make things like caviare sauce. But in a restaurant you've got much more simple food with a fresh approach. Roasted scallops, mozzarella salad, confit of duck leg. Quick fiery get-'em-ready-to-go starters. No messing about. At the Lancaster we served thick floury-based soups, turned out mousses, it was a rich sort of food. Then at Odette's it was all modern British with a Mediterranean influence.

So there I was at Odette's, a tiny restaurant compared to the hotels I'd been working in, and after a while the chef had a day off and told me to write the menu for the next day. I thought, 'Yeah, I can do it.' But I got in a lot of trouble at the beginning because my menus looked like hotel menus, not restaurant menus. I wrote something like 'steamed sea bass stuffed with salmon mousse in a saffron sauce'. I was told that was naff, that was hotel food. In the hotel it's terrines, things you can prepare beforehand, whereas in the restaurant it's good honest rustic food. They're serving good food, but haven't got the time to put eight little pieces of cucumber round a piece of salmon. Whereas in a hotel, you'll have all these noncy things on a plate. What they wanted in a small restaurant was fillet of beef, spinach, shallot sauce. Grilled peppers, rocket leaves, Parmesan. I'd never seen that. They didn't want cream and butter in their kitchen. It was all new to me: I didn't know what carpaccio was, at twenty-five years of age. I didn't know how to make pasta, didn't know how to grill peppers. Didn't know anything about that. And no bulk food. You were ordering one salmon today, perhaps another one tomorrow, not twenty at a time. At the same time I had loads more responsibility. Small kitchen, less staff. I was starting to do the ordering. Suddenly I'm not a chef who's working for someone else any more. If the head chef's off, I'm in charge. Then I'd work on the sauce, with everyone else working round me, on larder or veg, or just getting on with it. I became the leader – it was a first for me.

I learnt a lot there. At hotels you bought it, prepped it, and you had enough for three or four days: at a restaurant you buy it in that day, you prep it, sell it and do the same again the next day.

In a restaurant, there's what you called a 'roll-over' menu: if your fish supplier hasn't got what you've got on the menu, you have to write it out again. So you put something on and take something off. That's done every day. We'd do the menu before we went home, about half-past ten. The dates have to be changed daily on the menus, so if something isn't available you just leave it out. Here, where we're larger, we don't change that often; we probably change the menu every two or three months to coincide with seasonal availability of vegetables. The game season is coming up. I've got guinea fowl on at the moment, but I'm probably going to change to pheasant instead. And I might change to pigeon salad as a starter.

But I think that the massive gap between hotels and restaurants is starting to close now. People like Marco Pierre White have gone into hotels and that's why it's changed. A lot of hotels now have a restaurant run by a major chef, whose name people know, which brings the customers in. In the old days people would eat in hotels because, maybe, they'd heard of the hotel and it was big and flash and it seemed like something you did. These days if they eat at a hotel it's because they've heard of the chef, which is the same reason as they'd go to his restaurant. That the kitchen's part of a hotel is irrelevant, really. On the other hand hotels generally still lose out to restaurants, at least in London. Because there are so many restaurants in London now a lot of the customers come from the hotels, rather than their hotels feeding them. Hotel concierges recommend restaurants. One of our hospitality manager's jobs is to get to know the people in the hotel trade. Like so many other things, it's all down to who you know.

CHAPTER TEN

PRICES

In the end, whatever the alleged creativity that underpins its product, a restaurant is a business. And never more so than when that restaurant is part of a chain, as is increasingly the case today. A senior chef is as much a manager as a creative artist and his eye has to be as focused on the profit-and-loss accounting as it is on the food that he cooks.

Every restaurant sets a budget: you've got to make so many million a year. Over the year, your wage bill must be only so much, your food cost is say 28 per cent, your bar cost is say 28 per cent, your petty cash . . . That's the costs I'm talking about: if the food cost is 28 per cent, the profit is 72 per cent. You want to get costs down as far as possible, but it's silly to go too far. For instance if I managed to get costs down to 25 per cent this year, everyone would be pleased, but then they'd set that as the target and expect me to do it again the next year. It would be, 'Well done, Andrew, here's a fat bonus.' But if I couldn't do it the next year, no bonus. So you have to draw a realistic line.

My costs last week worked out at 26 per cent — which means 74 per cent profit. Now really I should be hitting 28 per cent. That's the target. I got 26 per cent, but it should be 28 per cent. A food cost of under 28 per cent is fantastic for me. Anything over, I need to find out why. At the moment I'm getting 23, 26, that's for the last two weeks. That's great, but over a whole year it might be 25.5 per cent and as I said the company will think, 'Right, next year we're going to make it 26.' Which means I've got to work even harder.

The company chairman sits down with the accountants and works out the targets over a year. Our year goes from July to July; that's an accountant's decision. They'll say, 'This is what we predict for next year.' So it will be, for example, £53,000 a week turnover in February, £57,000 per week in June, £56,000 per week in August. Come December, we're looking at £74,000 a week, because the private dining room will be sold out every day. So they set those targets for each week of the year. You can be up £2,000 one week, and down £2,000 the next. If we have bad January/Februarys, our budget will be knocked down to £53,000, but by the end of the month or the end of six months we might be on target. It all averages out.

My wage bill should be no more than 17 per cent of the turnover every week. So for what I need we should be taking £57,000. For example, I wasn't allowed to recruit any chefs in June. £57,000 is the turnover we're supposed to have per week at the moment. We're just about making it. We had two good weeks and then one bad one. It's good to have a good salon take, which ensures that we're over the weekly target. But we also have a private dining room. That brings in half a million a year. About £10,000 a week. If we've had a bad week it's usually because the private dining room hasn't been busy. In the restaurant and Rôtisserie, we have slow Mondays and Tuesdays, then there's mid-week, then Thursdays to Saturdays are the peak, then a quiet Sunday. Night time we get quite a lot of out-of-towners. Concierges at certain hotels send them in. We've got our own PR, our own hospitality manager. She's in charge of reception, selling the private dining room, and also of selling me. The

£57,000 we should be taking per week gets broken down. There's the wage bill, the bar supplies, the food, and so on. I buy my wine for cooking from the bar and they invoice me at the wholesale price. Each restaurant in the group has an individual bar stock, it's not ordered centrally.

In London a nice meal for four could cost as much as £200–£300. That's a week's wages for some people. You get a lot of people coming in off the M25 to eat in London. We have cards we get people to fill in, what they thought about the food and so on, and a lot of these people aren't from London, they're from the outskirts or from abroad. At Odette's we had people come in from Oxfordshire specially to eat at Odette's and they'd spend a lot of money. But others come into Soho, see Soho Soho – £15 for a piece of fish. Forget it. So they walk down to Chinatown instead. My father would never spend that kind of money on a meal. The teachers in Dagenham who my partner knows, they come into the West End. They can't pay that kind of money. They came in a couple of years ago, couldn't believe it was £13 for a steak.

I set the prices for the food, but it goes via head office, who have the final say. I control all the meats, the fish, buy all the goods, ingredients, garnishes, vegetables. I know whatever I'm buying can't be too expensive. I don't want it too cheap, but there must be a good profit margin in everything I buy. A 20 litre can of vegetable oil costs £15, but you don't make any money on that. Over the years you learn how to buy food and how to sell it. You learn that as you go along. You know it'll cost you say £4 for a side of salmon. You'll get eight portions out of that, at 50p each. I need to sell it for at least four times that. If it's a good-sized portion, I'll sell it for £12.50. And all of a sudden you've made so much money on a piece of fish. If I pay £10 for a side,

I'll get seven portions. I'll sell each portion for £12–£13 upstairs, and I'll get more portions out of one side downstairs, where I'll sell it for £9. So each side of salmon will fetch £85 plus. That's how I make my profit margin. If you're not making the margin you have to make changes. You look at what you're buying, who you're buying off, if someone else can bring in the same quality at cheaper prices. There's another, simpler way, and a lot of chefs will do it: just put a pound on the best-selling dishes. Admission: I once worked in a restaurant where the gross profit got so bad that we ended up using grey mullet (£1 a kilo) on the menu as 'Italian sea bass' (a fantasy fish). It made 95 per cent profit on each fillet we sold.

CHAPTER ELEVEN
EQUIPMENT

If a chef can be seen as a modern alchemist, turning the base metals of his raw materials into the gold of the finished dish, then, like his ancient predecessors, he requires the contemporary version of the alembic and the worm: the stoves and sinks, worktops and fridges, mixers and knives, and all the rest of the equipment that goes to furnish a modern restaurant kitchen. Like the brigade who use it, the range of equipment is flexible, varying from kitchen to kitchen and as ever to budget. A big new kitchen can cost many hundreds of thousands of pounds, and even a make-over comes in at around a quarter of a million. Not every restaurant offers such riches; chefs must and do adapt. Unsurprisingly, the quality of equipment is always improving, but the staples — a sharp knife, a hot flame and a sturdy pan — remain as central as ever.

In my upstairs kitchen, we're cooking for 130 in the restaurant plus anything up to another 100 in the salon when it's busy; that all comes from the same kitchen. Downstairs we have the Rôtisserie kitchen, serving another hundred plus. These two relatively small kitchens cram in as much equipment as they can. They're not ideal: there's a lot of stuff, set in at an awkward angle and terribly, terribly designed. The equipment has to be packed in tight. I've got two large walk-in fridges which cost in excess of £20,000, one blast chiller which cost £2,000—£3000, a double fridge upstairs, one service freezer, no bigger than a washing machine, a chest freezer downstairs in which we keep back-up *mise en place*, back-up bread basically. We've got four double fridges, one double stand-up fridge, two single stand-up fridges, one fridge with a set of pull-out drawers, one hot plate, a cooking range upstairs which has got two solid tops on and four gas-ring burners, which then gives us three stoves, three ovens I should say. We've got one small ring burner which sits at the side of the kitchen, on which we simmer our stock-pot: we use a hundred-litre stockpot to make stocks in every day. We've got one fryer upstairs which we rarely use, a double fryer downstairs. For the Rôtisserie downstairs we've just bought a four-ring burner — around about £10,000. We've got a salamander, that's a high-level grill, which we bought this year — that cost in excess of £2,000. There's a spit roast. The whole cooking range downstairs comes from a French company, which adds another problem because if the kit comes from France then you've got to send to France to get any spare parts, or even go there and pick them up. We've got a Hobart, a mixing machine, which costs £3,000, and the little bits and pieces that come with it cost a few hundred more, and obviously they sell you insurance to go with this equipment. Upstairs we've got a convector oven — it circulates the air throughout the cooking — which the pastry chef uses a lot. Otherwise he just comes and uses my stoves when he needs to, though he hardly ever does; he also uses a little heat ring, like a little heated plate.

Then there's the washing machines. One upstairs and another downstairs. Again you're talking £3,000– £4,000 pounds plus for branded machines and £400– £500 for chemicals, washing-up cloths, all that stuff. There's table settings. For the upstairs kitchen we've got about 250 main course plates and 150–200 starter plates. Soup bowls, we've only got about 45–50, cover plates on every table, salad bowls 150-plus. Downstairs they've got a different set of plates. Salts and peppers for every table, ashtrays, cups and saucers, the crockery bill is very expensive. We're in a group but our crockery is designed for us: 'Soho Soho' with a logo on the plates.

You've got a lot of catering companies that will provide you with your pots and pans, and all your crockery. There's about four big ones in London who are providing all this, Page's, Leon Jaeggi, a company called Parsley and Thyme, and Denny's, who do the aprons and the hats. It's all expanding. Look in the Yellow Pages — restaurant equipment, suppliers, clothing, knives — it's getting so big and obviously as the trade gets bigger and bigger, then more people start to think, 'Oh I'll open a shop that provides chefs' whites, or I'll open a shop that provides the cutlery and equipment, I'll open a huge company that'll provide the cooking equipment for restaurants and hotels . . .'

Sometimes designers come in to do a kitchen, sometimes it's the chef, usually a bit of both. Quag's, for instance, was designed by the chef who opened it. He planned it on the basis of the number of people that he wanted to serve. Obviously once a kitchen has been built as part of a restaurant it can't be changed, but you can and do change the equipment in that kitchen. As usual, you have to think about the budget. If you have the money available, whatever you want for a kitchen I'm sure you can get. My kitchen is eleven years old, but when people come to work for me, I say, 'Come and have a look in the kitchen — it's not paradise.' It's one of the things they have to take into consideration when they think about the job. And they can get paradise if they want. They can go to a brand-new kitchen and have the best equipment in the world. But in the end, just like the ingredients, it's not simply how much the kitchen costs, it's what you do with it.

But while that's true, I can't pretend that what you do in the kitchen, the dishes you can cook, isn't influenced by the equipment you have. One of the things I have to remember when I put together the menus is what the kitchen can handle. When you design a kitchen, you've got to have in mind what you'll be doing in it, you just write your menu around what you've got. But as well as having a lot more skilled people in kitchens, these days, the equipment itself is now manufactured to suit a particular dish. The technology has changed: ovens are different, better; the design of stove tops too. That sort of thing has changed the cooking all round. For instance, I don't think they had solid tops in kitchens a hundred years ago.

When you open a restaurant, you get given a budget, and equipment, large and small, obviously comes into that ongoing budget. There's a certain amount of money that you're allowed to spend on it now, depending on the size of the kitchen, and the overall budget that's been set for the year, the money they take every year, the turnover. Say you own twenty-two restaurants, some will take £3 million a year, some only £1.5 million. You have a yearly budget for your wage bill, for food and for kitchen equipment. There's also, if needed, a certain amount available for small kitchen equipment, about £100 a month. So you get your budget. And the idea is to spend that budget. If you could get what you want inside the budget, great. But if I only spend half of it, it's possible I won't get as much next year. I can spend about £20,000 on equipment this year. At a push, for that I can get two salamanders, top of the range. At the moment I can't glaze any-thing — there's no salamander to glaze it under. Last year we bought two brand-new walk-in fridges — they were £20,000 each. This year I want to buy a slicing machine, a sorbet machine, the salamanders. I need one more microwave. I need to get a shelf fitted to put one of the salamanders on. And the kitchen's full already, so when it comes to space to put it, we'll get rid of the old and bring in the new. As I said, the place *has* been open for eleven years now. Since I've been here it's been cleaned up, and it's been changed as well, so some of the equipment looks brand new. But it's not just cooking equipment: I still need brand-new wall tiles in the whole of my upstairs kitchen, and that would be £2,000 on top.

As well as the regular stock-takes on food, you sometimes have to do stock takes on equipment as well. I don't do it here, but one restaurant I worked at you had to do a one or two monthly stock-take on all the equipment you had: pots, pans, terrines, plates, knives, forks, baking trays, roasting trays, stainless steel bowls for your service, measuring jugs, whisks, ladles, spoons, sieves, colanders, a chinois [a fine sieve], all this equipment costs so much money, and you had to do stock-takes every year because there were people nicking everything.

When you actually get down to putting a kitchen together there are a lot of people involved. We've got seven or eight different maintenance groups and kitchen equipment fitters who provide the Group with what's required if we're going to open a new restaurant. They're the same people who supplied us in the restaurants that have been built or opened in the last so many years and they come along and they'll design the kitchen that you want and they'll provide the equipment necessary. But as a chef you have to live with the fact that while a lot of groups will have plenty of money up front to spend on a kitchen, there's plenty of others that prefer to build the kitchen up at minimum expense.

The cook's first tool is the knife. There's loads of other equipment, but the main tool is the knife. Chefs have their own knives and they buy those out of their wages. (In Australia they get an allowance for it, I believe, but not in England.) You will very, very, very rarely go into a kitchen where they provide the knives for you. Being a chef must be like being a joiner or a chippie or something: you've got your own equipment and you don't want other people to use it; you look after it yourself and you sharpen it yourself; it's yours, it belongs to you. And the longer you're in the trade, the more knives you pick up and the ones that are older and older – you always look back on those knives and say, 'Oh, I had that knife when I was working at so-and-so.' I only had a certain number of knives when I went to Gleneagles, but I was very lucky to find a lad who was really desperate for money and he sold me four top-quality knives for £10. These days my knife case probably averages out at about £200-plus worth of knives, but some of them were bought years ago so they're not top price; now if you go and buy a knife you probably spend £30–£40 on one. What are the best knives? It depends – all chefs have favourites, you'll get chefs who like to buy Gustav, Emil & Ern, chefs who like to buy Japanese knives, there's Sheffield Steel, Victorinox, Sabatier, There are fashions in knives. Fifteen years ago it was Sabatier, now you've got Chinese knives, Japanese knives coming in – there's lots of different types.

Basically you need eight to ten different knives: a palette knife, a peeler, a cook's knife, a filleting knife, a parer knife (which is like a vegetable knife), a boning knife, a carving knife and you need a steel to sharpen them. You just have to build up your collection: buy 'em, pinch 'em, lose 'em, pinch 'em back. You probably get one as a Christmas present now and again. You'll find when you go in kitchens that a lot of chefs they've got their names on the knives, they've got sticky tapes round the knives basically to say, 'That's my knife, see that sign on it, says it's my knife, so it's my knife. And leave it alone.'

A professional stove costs £15,000– £20,000 and more. Stoves can last for ever as long you keep them clean all the time. The reality is you should get a good five years out of a stove, some-times even longer. But they're worked very hard: seventeen hours a day. Seven in the morning till twelve o'clock at night. What you want from a good stove is heat, adjustability, and you want it to light first time all the time. That'll only happen if you look after it, replacing the thermo-couple regularly, getting it serviced regularly. Ours are serviced every six months, I think. If something does break down it can be difficult to get the parts – it sometimes takes up to three weeks. The pilot valves on both griddles broke once when I was away. So, crisis. We either wait three weeks to get new parts fitted or put in a brand-new range, costing £10,000–£12,000 – because we're going to lose a lot of money in three weeks without the griddles.

In a big restaurant in the West End, the kitchen was refur-bished for £250,000. If you spend that much, all the ovens are going to be better, all the pilots on the ovens will be fixed so that they don't start falling off. The on–off button doesn't fall off, either, which they do with all the use. Small things – but vital. You'll get griddles, up-to-date salamanders, ring burners, fryers (not just your average fryer but an actual system where the fryers are all built into the design) so that the whole worktop is one straight line and the fryers are actually fitted into the gaps. At Soho Soho ours is just a wheelabout stand-up fryer; go along to a big kitchen and you'll find that the fryers are built into the worktop and then you'll open a door so the oil can be emptied and so on; it just looks a lot neater as well and it's a lot more workable. The only thing is that you can't wheel your fryer round to the other kitchen when the one there breaks down. Then there's the canopies to go above the stoves; you've got to pay a lot of money for those too. And the extractor systems to help the canopy do its job. To get one of those you're talking hundreds of thousands of pounds.

Most stoves are put together as a range, which is a variety of linked equipment all built in one area. On the left you'll maybe have some solid tops and in the middle you could have a bain-marie; next to that you could have a chargriddle, then another solid top, then a four-ring burner, and finally another bain-marie. You just build it up as you want it. The designers don't actually sell all this in one big lump, you choose what you want and buy it individually, but they make it into one unit. Each stove on the range has its own oven.

Solid tops are only found in professional kitchens. They're just a solid piece of metal that covers the whole stove and underneath there's one big burner or two small ones — it makes a difference in the level of heat from the outside to the middle. You can't sit your pans on the corner of a normal stove with separate burners — they might tip over. A single burner just gives you a one-off power, the flame is just where it is; with the solid top, the heat spreads all around it and you can move the pans wherever you need to. In the middle of a solid top is a removable ring with the burner underneath it and when you take the ring out of the solid top you get the full power of the heat at the bottom of the pan — otherwise it just spreads heat evenly all around.

Nearly all restaurant kitchens run on gas. There's the odd small kitchen where they've got a solid top which runs on electricity, and it doesn't get hot until you put your pan on it.

These are more like the stoves you might find in a private house: you put your pan on it and it starts to heat up, but until you put your pan on it it stays cool. But the majority of kitchens stick with gas. We use twenty-two separate gas outlets — upstairs, in the Rôtisserie and so on. Every pilot light lights a ring, and we have twenty-two pilot lights going every day. It makes for a very big gas bill. It also throws out an enormous amount of heat. The gas pipes that connect the kitchen stoves to the mains are a lot bigger than normal — maybe two inches instead of the usual half-inch — because with more than one stove to feed the pressure has to be maintained along the full run of the range. If the pipe isn't broad enough, the pressure isn't there. While the stove nearest the start of the pipe will get plenty of gas, and get the heat you want, the one at the far end won't. The alternative is to go back to the mains and run a separate pipe to each stove, but that takes up far too much space. So that pipe and the pressure it delivers have to be the way you want them.

At the end of our range we have this small burner that heats the stockpot. Again, there's a choice: you can buy a stockpot that's just your average basic hundred-litre pot, which can sit on a small burner — which is the way we do it — or you can do what they did at Gleneagles and have boilers, like vats. With these you can turn the temperature down and you can use them for stocks, soups and stews. They are the best thing for soups and stocks, because, as we've found loads of times, if you're trying to make a crab bisque in a boiler and somebody turns the heat up by mistake, the bottom burns straight away.

Some kitchens have what's called a brat pan. Brat pans can be anything up to two foot long by a foot wide. They've got high sides, about 8 to 10 inches deep. At the hotel I first worked in when I came to London they had about four brat pans and a griddle, a makeshift griddle which they fitted into the brat pan to seal the meat. It got red hot once you turned it on and you put oil in it and then you sealed off all the meats for parties. It's like a frying pan, but the biggest frying pan you'll ever see. There's all sorts of things you can do with a brat pan – you can use it for soups, for casseroles, for bisques, for sealing meat, for roasting fish shells. You can use it as a blanching pot, or you can just fill it with water and salt and use it for cooking all your fish. They've got pressure timers on them so you can pull the lid down, set the timer and it steams the food. At Quag's, they cooked all the shellfish in them in the morning, and then in the afternoon they used them to make a bisque and then the bisque would come off, and then later on, before they went home at night, they'd use them to make stock and leave the stock on overnight.

We've got sixteen fridges in total. Various sizes. In a kitchen you'll find a few different types of fridge. The first type is a bench fridge, which basically combines the bench-top that you work on and the fridge underneath it all in one. A double bench fridge costs from about £3,000 to £7,000, depending on size, worktop included. They're never more than about three foot to three foot four inches high. Which means you've got a worktop, and underneath are fridges with normal open-and-shut doors. You just open that door and you can see exactly what you've got in the fridge – all your sauces, the *mise en place*. Whatever section you're on, you don't have to keep running back to a big fridge to get the food you need because everything for that service that day is there ready under the worktop. Bench fridges are always stainless steel, including the worktop. It's the most hygienic work surface: you can't have wooden tops like you would at home. Steel is obviously easier to clean and it's hygienic. You get all these chemicals for keeping it clean.

Other bench fridges have drawers instead of doors. So you might have half your fridges with a door that you open to get inside, and the other half with drawers that you pull out. It all makes for better organisation: you know that your meat garnish is on the top shelf and your salad garnish is on the middle one – so you just pull that drawer out as you're doing the garnish for your dish and it's all there. The point is to arrange your fridge so that it's as easy and quick to use as possible because the last thing you want to be doing is opening three or four doors every service to find out where something has been put. So we try to make it so that you know exactly what's going to be in every fridge. Each fridge is set out so that if somebody goes and works in that section, they know where everything is in that fridge because it's going to be where it's always kept. Or, if you don't know, you can ask the main chef on the section because most of them will know how it's been sorted out. As well as the bench fridges there's also a service fridge for your back-up *mise en place* – because you've always got to assume that some of the bench fridges are going to break down.

The biggest fridge is the walk-in fridge itself, which, like everything else, depends on the size of the building. At Gleneagles they had an enormous walk-in dairy, fruit and veg fridge, which was probably bigger than the kitchen that I work in now. (This was the fridge that was also used for punishment – if you messed up, the senior sous chef would take you inside and make you clean it out and he'd close the door while you were doing it. All your rubbish had to be piled in one corner and then, when he opened the door, he expected it to be spot-on, no boxes, all sorted out, all on the right shelves and in the right places.) But it's down to space and some places simply don't have the room for a walk-in fridge or a really big freezer. They use a chest freezer, which is no different from the one you might have at home or perhaps, if there's a bit more room, a stand-up freezer, which looks the same as a stand-up fridge, about twelve foot high.

All the major equipment – the fridges and the stoves – is serviced every six months. Servicing catering equipment costs millions and millions a year. For every piece of kitchen equipment, there's someone to say, 'If it breaks down, I'll fix it.' We have electricians on maintenance contracts and they earn a *lot* of money for what they do. Conran restaurants have engineers on site in all their restaurants – and they always have jobs to do. There are electrical maintenance companies all round the outskirts of London: it's great business for them, thousands of restaurants in London using all this equipment. We signed up with two companies at the beginning of this year to do all our maintenance.

The fridges come from Williams, which supplies fridges for restaurants and bars all over the country – it's a huge company. They also service them. Like the stoves, the fridges are worked hard and they break down. Pressure valves go, pumps fail, whatever; they overheat. To get a replacement part for most of them is expensive: you're talking about £200 at a time. But, whatever you pay, it takes time to order and deliver parts, and in the meantime you've got fridges not working. So you need to keep up your maintenance contracts all the time. All of which eats into the budget. And when they come along to fix the fridge or the cooker, they'll invoice you for the time they've spent there and they'll also invoice you for the car park round the corner where they've parked. A call-out costs £35 plus. Of course, sometimes the fridges go wrong for other reasons: like a power cut. We have some back-up, but if the electricity stays off the food starts to go off and you can't afford to start serving stuff that might give people food poisoning. When that happens you have to empty the fridges, toss away the food, and do a huge re-order from the ground up. It's a nightmare.

Maintenance is part of the budget like everything else. This year we're only allowed to spend £10,000 on it. The Group specifies the company we can use and they'll service our fridges twice a year. It'll probably cost three grand to get them serviced each time, so there's six grand out of the ten spent on fridge maintenance alone. If they service them twice a year obviously they should be in working order for six months at a time, but if anything else goes wrong in between there's nothing you can do about it. If your fridge breaks down and it's the best fridge you've got and it's the most important, you've got to get it fixed. And that's when the maintenance companies will come along and start piling the pounds on. You have to check them very carefully, otherwise they'll just charge you whatever they can get away with.

There's also a lot of business in restaurants for plumbers when things go wrong. And for drain-clearing firms like Dynorod. They're always around kitchens. I've been in a kitchen where all the tubes and all the waste pipes underneath the kitchen were blocked with a mixture of the food that was being whizzed down the plughole and all the fat that had been poured down there and had set hard. The result was that all the drains had backed up – the kitchen was flooded, there were turds floating around in there and everybody was getting involved in getting all that water out, while Dynorod were trying to sort something out. Horrible. And totally unhygienic.

* * *

One of the great innovations over the last few years has been the blast chiller. It doesn't actually freeze the food, but cools it down very, very fast. Almost instantly. You take your soup or beef, or whatever you've got that's hot, and you put it into the blast chiller and just press 'blast' and it chills everything down as quickly as possible. It keeps the food fresh and it stops the cooking process immediately. For instance, when you do a duck leg confit, as soon as you take the duck leg out you put it into the chiller and it blasts it straight away. Then you can put it into a normal fridge and when you want a duck confit to send away you put it into the oven cold and let it heat up thoroughly and crisp the skin. If you took the duck confit out of the pan, thinking it was cooked just right, and left it to cool down naturally, on an open shelf, you run the chance of food poisoning. Not only that, but from the cooking point of view it would still be cooking as it's cooling down and it could overcook. So again the blast chiller helps because it stops everything dead – it can't carry on cooking.

These days the law says that every restaurant has to have a blast chiller and it's definitely one of the reasons that food poisoning's getting more and more rare. It's one of the good things that the environmental health people have done. On the one hand blast chilling cuts down the chance of food going off, and at the same time a blast chiller helps you out when you get complaints – you know the food was cooked and then chilled straight away. You have to keep records of all this information – when you put things into the chiller you have to record the temperature – which means that when I get rung up by someone from the Group to say that there's been a complaint and they tell me what the person who's complaining ate, I've got my records to prove I cooled it down straight away – what temperature it went in at and the temperature when it came out. Say the problem is with some pork. When you cook pork it's got to be cooked to over 70–80° C, and you'll have recorded that it was over that temperature when it went into the chiller, which means it was properly cooked, and when you brought it out it was under 3° C, so it was most definitely cold. That record proves that the pork couldn't have been the problem. The blast chiller has various uses, but there's no doubt that one of them is to save face when you get food-poisoning complaints.

When I started out they didn't have blast chillers. I worked at one restaurant where they used to put the soups outside in the car park to cool down, or by an open window, or simply stuck them straight in the fridge. None of which was exactly good for health and safety. When I went to Gleneagles eleven or twelve years ago, they didn't have a chiller; they had about twelve massive ovens – four huge roasting ovens, and eight convector ovens – plus all the ovens on the ranges; they had two brat pans, four boilers, all this equipment making all that food – and no blast chiller. They didn't exist in those days. Looking back, I wonder how they survived and, just as important, how did they get away with it? But things like that just weren't talked about then, and I didn't really think about it myself until I got to Quaglino's and came across a blast chiller for the first time.

You get jackets supplied, a fresh one every day, but a lot of chefs I know have to buy their trousers. There's all these different types of chefs' trousers at the moment, black and white trousers, checked, blue and white, a very fine check like gingham. I don't really know why, maybe it's just a style . . . It's a uniform – and it's been around a long time. These days there's a new fashion – some chefs now wear the 'I'm head chef' black trousers. The first time I saw it was at Gleneagles: the executive chef wore black trousers and black buttons on his jacket and everybody else had white buttons and the usual blue check trousers. Now it's got very popular; you get these pretentious wankers who walk round with black trousers and black buttons . . . A lot of head chefs have their name embroidered on their jackets. I used to. I don't now, although it's not just showing off, it's useful for identification: when someone approaches you in a busy hotel or restaurant and they walk past you and they know, 'Oh it's the head chef. Hi, how're you doing? . . .'

Laundry is now a big thing as well. You've got companies fighting it out for your business just as much as the fruit and veg suppliers do. Our laundry bill is probably in excess of £100,000 a year easily – that's just one medium-sized restaurant – napkins, tablecloths, chefs' trousers, chefs' whites, aprons, tea towels, oven cloths, glass cloths; a lot of the bill gets spent on tablecloths – that's the main cost. Quite a lot of restaurants or restaurant/ brasseries – they don't use all the tablecloths and so on that you get in a traditional place. Which means they probably have nicer flowers and everything else round the building because you've got more money to spend on flowers if you're spending less on laundry. And flowers are a lot cheaper than laundry.

CHAPTER TWELVE

ENVIRONMENTAL HEALTH

Soups in the car park, cockroaches round the fridge, spit in the soup — the nature of kitchens does not automatically promote the best standards of hygiene and cleanliness. No one would suggest that chefs actively advocate dereliction of health and safety, but the fact remains that certain aspects of culinary preparation are, as it were, less than appetising. The policing of standards is in the hands of the local council, more especially its environmental health officers. Pilloried on occasion as 'drain-sniffers', the EHOs probably save not a few of us from suffering after-effects from our meal that are even more unappealing than the bill.

The environmental health officers' job is to make sure your kitchen is working to the right standard of health and safety, and if you want to operate as a restaurant kitchen you have to have a certificate from them. They'll come to you with a list and say, 'We haven't seen each other before, we'll write a full report on your kitchen.' They've got a lot of power, but a lot of them are jobsworths and they've hardly even seen a kitchen before. In the end, though, I'm quite pleased for them to come in checking. They'll say, 'You need this, you need that,' and that gives me ammunition to go to the boss and say, 'I've been told we've got to do this. If we don't, we'll be closed down.' Though I don't think they can close you down right then. You get a severe warning first.

Of course, standards of hygiene differ. One place will do everything, another virtually nothing. In the Royal Lancaster you had to check fridge temperatures every morning, all over the building, as you do at Soho Soho now. Then again, at two p.m. You check the temperature, that it's working, not too hot or cold. You're insured against a fridge full of off food. A lot of big hotels and kitchens have their own electricians to sort that out. In the Royal Lancaster there were a lot of health and safety rules and everyone had to know about the hygiene rules. Everyone had to have a hygiene certificate: you went on a course.

When the EHOs come in, the first thing they do is check all the fridges. Then they go to your service fridges, check how you've got the food on your shelves, to make sure meat and fish are not mixed up together. They'll come at eight a.m. and just watch everything you do. Some of what they ask for is a legally binding requirement, some of it isn't. Some of their advice helps you, the rest is jobsworth.

They don't just check the food, but things like the tiles, the dishwashing system, the wire scrubbers – those little wires can get stuck in a handle, and might later fall back into food – and any other potential risk areas in the kitchen that might not be controlled properly. They'll watch everything you do at a service, then say, 'But he had a hot stainless container with his knives in at the start of service and as he was getting through service it was getting dirty.' And they expect you to stop everything, change the water, or put a sanitiser in it. A lot of chefs in private places would just tell them to fuck off, but when you're in a company you have to set an example. But still, if you've got a full service at lunchtime, you can't go round thinking of washing your knife box. The EHOs don't understand that, they just advise you to do it.

We use the right chopping boards for the different foods, and we label and date everything, so we use it in rotation. We've got the blast chiller to cool food down. We've got a temperature gauge now. Beef you want to cook rare. So you record the temperature of the beef when it went into the chiller and again when you take it out. If you put it in warm, it must come out cold. We used to put big boxes of chips in the chiller, but now we put the chips on the stairs for a couple of hours to cool down because the heat of the chips would blow the fuse in the chiller. Eggs, pork and chicken in the chiller, all have to be recorded.

The sorts of thing that come out of a visit are quite small, but they add up. The last time they came round the EHO decided there were quite a lot of problems. All the plastic containers needed the right labels, and when the container was empty that label had to be scraped off and a new one put on. Some things weren't well enough covered. The big containers in the fridge with onions in should have had a lid on. Even unpeeled carrots should have had a lid. The eggs in the salad fridge had to be moved to the meat and fish fridge. No cardboard boxes are allowed in fridges, apart from egg trays. If you put eggs out in the fridge, they draw the smells of everything else, but if they're in a box, that doesn't happen. All the big containers in the bottom of the fridges had to be on a raised level. You can't have boxes of butter in the fridge, it all has to come out of the boxes. On the shelves, it's cooked meat on the top, raw meat in the middle and fish on another shelf, very well wrapped, if under the meat. Raw meat mustn't drip on to anything. Fish on the bottom. All our fish is in clingfilm or in containers with lids. You know that a lot of the things they ask are over the top. I know what's going on here, I control it, accidents won't happen; but for them it's got to be correct, be perfect. So they'll always have something to say. You do your best. In the end it's a case of: 'This is the space I've got, I keep it as best I can.'

Not all visits are prearranged. A few weeks ago Westminster Council popped in, unannounced, at half-past five at night, wanting to look round the kitchen. They have the right to do that. So the EHO came into the kitchen with his white jacket and his little thermometer and checked all the fridges, the space in between the shelves [for air circulation], checked what was in there, whether it was covered, that the food was on the right shelves. He checked the fish fridges. Then he looked at the tiles, the extractor fans, my main big fridges, at the back stairwell — checking whether it was slippery or cracked. He went to the staff changing room, to check working conditions. He was looking for circumstances that would encourage mice, cockroaches, snakes or anything else. When he'd finished he said, 'Not bad, but your changing room leaves a bit to be desired.' I said, 'Thank you very much, I can now report this to the company.' I was quite pleased really.

We follow their advice if we can. It costs the company money every time we get a visit. On their advice we bought a thermostat for the blast chiller, bought the coloured chopping boards, bought plastic cups for staff tea and coffee, got rid of all the glasses. We also bought rubber mats for the potwash area. The KPs were putting cardboard boxes down there and if they're on the wet floor they could slip. We've done quite a lot. The only thing we need now are the little stands to put food on in the fridges.

The bottom line with food is that you've got to keep it fresh, you've got to serve it quickly and keep it refrigerated until you do serve it. In a kitchen people should work as if they're being constantly watched by health inspectors.

There's all sorts of things, not directly to do with cooking or food, that can cause problems. If your fire doors aren't closed when you get a fire inspection, you can get shut down straight away. Our back door's a fire door. Obviously that's always closed. All the other doors in the building are fire doors and have to be kept closed. You can't prop them open with an extinguisher or something. If your back area is blocked with boxes or oil drums when they turn up, you can get a heavy fine or even be closed down. That's a fire hazard: blocking the exit.

They'll check that every staff member has a hygiene certificate: that proves you know how to work in a kitchen, how to clean a bench. We send everyone on a company hygiene course. They do check that you're wearing a hat. A lot of chefs would wear hats anyway because they want to. The old chefs all wore tall hats, but they just get in the way. The taller the hat, the higher your position, that was what it was all about. Then they brought in the skull caps, but you had to wash them yourself, and no matter what you did you ended up with a line around your head. It's meant to be hygienic, though of course the front-of-house staff don't wear hats and they're serving the food. They also check storage – no glasses allowed in the kitchen, only plastic cups and bottles. If you bring a big bottle of wine to pour into the stockpot, once it's empty it goes straight out again. We have a dry store at the back of the upstairs kitchen where part-empty bottles go. You *can* have a bottle of wine in your kitchen, but they don't want it on a high shelf in case it falls and smashes and there's glass everywhere.

Then there's vermin. London has a massive vermin prob-lem: it's a huge city and you can't escape. Different areas have different vermin: St John's Wood's full of cockroaches; in Soho it's mice and pharaoh ants – tiny brown ants. Pharaoh ants have been around for years. If you get them you call up the extermi-nator and they clear them out in one go. You do see mice in the West End, though I've never seen any rats, although I have no doubt they're around. Soho gets full of garbage between mid-night and five a.m. when the binmen come and take it all away. That's when the vermin come out.

Given the possible problems with vermin we also have Pest Control coming round all the time. They're different from the EHO. They'll set traps. One company have a gel they put down which attracts the cockroaches. What roaches like in restaurants is places like behind the washing machines, where all the steamy heat is. Put down the gel, it kills them off. But they will come in. You'll never get rid of all of them. Pest Control set traps for mice with poisoned bait, and catch quite a lot. But how big a hole does a mouse need? This is Soho: very old, hundreds of eating places, bars, whatever, loads of rubbish coming out of every one. It's a battle, and maybe you don't always win. What you've got to do is prove you're fighting that battle, which we do, and all I can say is I keep my kitchen clean.

But whatever the EHO do, it doesn't mean every kitchen comes up to the proper standards. I went to this kitchen once which was filthy. They had such a disgusting kitchen it was unbelievable. The fridges were terrible. The equipment they were using, stoves, hotplates – all the knobs had come off, they were turning them on with a knife or a pair of pliers; there were wires hanging everywhere; stale oil was left dirty in the fryer; boxes were piled up everywhere. They had boxes in fridges, no labels – they had absolutely nothing. The chefs were just work-ing for the money – they didn't care about it being clean. They were only worried about whether the owner might come down and go mad because it was dirty. Which he never did. Then he got a food-poisoning complaint from a wedding party: thirty people. Twelve of them went down with poisoning. Twenty-four had had the same dish, half became sick.

Even rubbish collections in London are very carefully monitored now. All these rules. If you get Westminster Council to do it, you have to buy sticky labels off them and make sure every bag goes out with a label on. There's a £500 fine if you forget the label and they know where it's come from. You get charged 25p for every sticker that goes on a bin sack. We use about 120 bags a week. Which is about £1,500 a year. These days we've dropped the council and have a firm, EnviroWaste, that takes away all our bin sacks. We crush all the stuff into special bins. There's the pigswill bins, box bins, bottle bins. We pay someone to collect the pigswill bins and empty them and take it away, and we pay some-one to pick up all the bottles and rubbish every morning, between five and six, in a big refuse truck and put all the bins back. This is a new idea and only certain restaurants are using them, these wheel-in/wheel-out plastic compactor things. You wheel it in, put all your bags in, crush them, and when it's full, wheel it out and put an empty one in. Someone who has his own key comes in in the morning, empties them and puts them back. You should come into work and all the bins be empty again. But given the amount of rubbish we generate, if you've got stuff that's not been taken away that day, you're in trouble. Over the Christmas period it gets very difficult: you just hope they're going to turn up.

The food waste goes for pigswill. The pigswill man comes about eight a.m., takes it away, leaves empty bins again. Our man picks up around 140 bins every day from West End restaurants. The swill gets taken away and after the contents of the bins have been sorted out to get rid of non-edible rubbish, such as tinfoil, cardboard, food wrapping and so on, it's 'cooked' in vats by steam. The resulting pigswill gets eaten by 1,400 pigs, who are fed it through a pipe. The bins are then boil-washed daily.

Every restaurant has to have a first aider, someone on duty at all times who's done the first aid course. Hotels and big groups are very strict on this and make sure you do your courses. But some small restaurants don't even think about it. We've got one lady who organises all the courses: for interviewing, first aid, health and hygiene, management, chefs' training courses. Once you've done the first aid course, you have to go back for a refresher after two or three years. The courses are expensive. St John Ambulance are involved and make a lot of money out of it.

When you're under pressure, you go too fast and you can accidentally cut your finger. I was cutting into my fingers, right into the centre, back in my prawn cocktail days. When I was doing my lemons, I'd go through the lemon and cut my finger. Chefs are under pressure and tired. But on the whole you carry on working. If I get cut, I just put clingfilm round it. Some chefs cry and say, 'I've got to go home', but not often. I've seen chefs burn themselves really badly, but they carry on working.

So you have to have first aid training, health and hygiene training and food hygiene training. And you have to be trained to handle your cleaning chemicals. They're all downstairs in one cupboard, away from the food. The area rep of the company comes in every so many months and goes through all the chemicals with the staff, including the kitchen porters. They've got to know how to use the chemicals, know what's dangerous. You get D9s, D2s, D1s. D9 is the highest toxicity – that would be an oven cleaner, just basically acid. At Gleneagles the D9 was vinegar. The commis chefs had to stay behind and clean the stoves before they went home, all the solid tops – no night cleaners there – and what they'd be doing is putting vinegar on it to clean it.

Keeping up with all this health stuff costs, but it's nothing compared to the things that can go wrong if people complain about food poisoning. I don't think there's insurance for that. We haven't had complaints of food poisoning for a long, long time, but there are complaints about all sorts of other things. Recently we had a fellow who had carpaccio, which is raw beef thinly sliced. I'm sure you can't get food poisoning off it because it's not cooked. Anyway this chap ate half of it, then told the waiter he was feeling sick and dizzy. He ordered his main course, then said he couldn't hold his knife and fork properly, he was really ill. But they still stayed for dessert. So all of a sudden he's ill from eating carpaccio. He kept ringing back about it, but we haven't seen a letter from his doctor yet to know how ill he was.

Then there was a lady we had in not so long ago. She sent us a letter saying she'd had a superb meal, superb service, but she ate a new potato and, when she bit into it, it burnt her mouth. On antibiotics for a burnt mouth. And she said the potatoes must have been cooked in a microwave because they were cold on the outside. We do have a microwave, but we never cook potatoes in it.

Another time a fellow sent his salmon back in the Rôtisserie – an escalope of salmon that he and his friend ate. His friend ate all of his, but this chap, he said his tasted off. So he ordered chicken instead. As it happened the chef was in the middle of service, really busy, really under pressure and because of this the bloke had to wait quite a while for his chicken. He ate all that, paid up and left. Then he rang up and complained that he was sick with food poisoning.

These are typical complaints and whether you agree with them or not, you have to make sure they get dealt with properly. To help you there are three or four food complaint companies which regulate hygiene complaints in restaurants. What happens after a customer makes a complaint is that first he leaves his name and number and explains just what he ate, which can also be checked out on his bill. We then fill out a form giving details of who we bought the food from, how and when it was cooked, and we pass it on to one of these external regulators. The sous chefs get lumbered with this, writing out the recipe, the ingredients, the cooking method, the blast chilling, the reheating – everything that goes to put out one dish. The company then gets in touch with the customer and gathers information from them. The restaurant's job is to prove that they have met the regular standard practice in cooking the meal that has been served. This gets passed on to the regulator. After that the customer either gets a letter saying that everything was in order and their complaint has no foundation, or, if there is a justifiable complaint, it can go to court. If you're a customer you're advised to make a complaint to one of these companies.

But you can't always trust the people who are complaining. Sometimes they're just after a free meal or compensation. Not long ago a guest came into the restaurant, ordered an omelette and immediately sent it back. It was overcooked. We made him another one. Back it came again. This time we found a large chunk of metal inside the omelette. It couldn't possibly have come off any piece of kitchen equipment. But before the manager could go over to him to discuss the situation he was already on his feet, shouting, 'If you don't give me five hundred pounds cash at once, for me to keep my mouth shut, I'll report you to the environmental health and the papers.' It didn't work. The manager threw him out – we never heard another word about it. He must have been doing it all round the West End. Maybe sometimes he even got lucky.

CHAPTER THIRTEEN
THE HEAD CHEF

The image of the chef, carefully nurtured by a decade's increasingly fascinated media, currently ranges from the laddish accessibility of a Jamie Oliver – all jokey one-liners and chirpy Cockney sparrer-isms – to the wayward genius – personal psychoses muted only by the brilliance of their dishes – of a Gordon Ramsay or Marco Pierre White. Delia Smith or the Galloping Gourmet may in their times have cut greater swathes and sold more books but they are cooks, not chefs, geared to the household and not the professional kitchen. The militarism of the kitchen, seen already in its disciplined top-down hier-archy, confers substantial power upon a head chef. Like any such power, it is all too open to abuse. It is, on the whole, a self-perpetuating approach. Like the veterans of a tough military 'boot camp', senior chefs (at least the male variety) tend to the belief that 'I survived – and it made me the chef I am.' Rarely do they appreciate the irony of such bravado pronouncements. While writing this book a commis working in a Michelin-level restaurant was 'branded' by his head chef wielding a hot palette knife. The response from Andrew's kitchen was 'He probably had it coming.' Women chefs, it is generally agreed, manage to sidestep this culinary macho, which is a product, perhaps, of the image, as Andrew has noted, of being put down as 'a pansy' for wanting to cook. The professional kitchen, and the professional chef, are tough: both emotionally and physically. Simply standing up on your feet for a long 'double' (eight a.m. to three-thirty p.m., five p.m. till well after

161

midnight) is exhausting. Varicose veins are a classic chef's problem. The heat of the stoves, the endless noise – human and mechanical – is wearing. The sheer pressure of preparing food, both to a consistent quality and nightly quantity, is draining. Adrenalin can only compensate so far.

Being a chef requires total dedication, care, skill, time and thought just for starters. These are what will take you from being a commis to your first job as head chef in the first kitchen that is truly yours.

Once you get in the kitchen it's not about what the owners are like, or the image of the restaurant, or anything like that; it's about what you make of the place, and what you do yourself. If you don't get it together, if you're not up to scratch, whatever your problem, it's your fault. No one else's. But if you've got confidence in yourself and know what you want to do and what's right from wrong, then you'll do it.

Just getting a head chef's job is important in itself. Not everyone appreciates that. There are plenty of chefs out there who don't realise how lucky they are to be in a head chef's job. They can't all pick and choose. It happens to everyone. A while back a friend came to me and said, 'Well I don't know if I want to work, I might go to the agency and get out of my restaurant.' He'd only been there three months. It took me half an hour to say to him, 'Look, you've got a good job, you're a head chef, you've got a good restaurant. At the end of it, all you have to remember is that if the place isn't working right, it's your fault, because what happens in the kitchen area is all down to how you make it.' He thought about it and now he's saying, 'Yeah, you're right.' A lot of people walk into a place, think it's all wrong, and think, 'No, I'm not doing this. I'll go and try somewhere else.'

But what happens is that they try somewhere else and again they're thinking, 'No this isn't right' – the point is that it's not the place, it's the person. You have to get experience, which you do by working somewhere for two years, three years at the most. Then you leave and get a better job by going somewhere new and you do this over and over again until you get to the top. Of course, when you get somewhere new it's difficult: it takes you six months to get used to it, and the first six months you're thinking, 'Shall I stay? Shall I go?' but having already had that experience of moving around through different restaurants and so on, you're going to know what you want to do. So you don't just leave. You just have to bide your time, you just have to wait a little and then you get what you want. I've always done that, but not everyone does. I think the people who have ups and downs are the people who are impatient and think it's all everybody else's fault. That's not right: they have to look at themselves and think, 'Maybe it's me . . .' In the end the old cliché's true: it's down to you and if you can't stand the heat – get out.

Being a head chef is a twenty-four-hour a day commitment. You can't just put it away at the end of a shift or even the end of the day. You've got to go into the kitchen and all day you've got to think about who's thinking what, who's doing what and what they want; and at the same time what you're going to do and how you're going to do it, and to do it right and to keep doing it, on and on and on. Chefs who aren't sure about being in the trade should stay out of it. You really have to decide whether you want to do it, and it doesn't mean you've got to go out and work in a Michelin-star restaurant, you've simply got to go out and do what you can do and put your full commitment into it. If you think you want to work in a kitchen but you can't put that full commitment into it – even if you're still working in the kitchen

— well, then it really screws you up, you really have a hard time. It's like any other job: you're somewhere where you don't want to be, and because of that you're only going to be putting in half your effort. And if there are others around who are putting in 100 per cent effort then you're not just unhappy in yourself, but more importantly you're the weak link in their chain, you're letting everyone down. That's even more true when you get to be head chef, because as a head chef you need your team to be behind you 100 per cent.

You do take your job home, it's always on your mind. You're sitting watching TV, say, but it comes back to you: What parties have we got next week? Who's working? Who have I got to speak to? What do I have to sort out? Have I done the costing sheets for my new dishes? Will this work? Did I ring the butcher Friday night? Did I do this before I went home? Did I do that? You can't really switch off, you're just obsessed with it. It's different for junior chefs. They don't have that responsibility. They work hard, but when they stop they stop. They love what they're doing, but when they leave the kitchen that's it. They go out, have fun, they can forget about the job. But as you go up through your career, that starts to change. All of a sudden, one day, you're in charge of a section in the kitchen and you have to start thinking. Not just about cooking, but about managing that section. When you get to the top, you've got to think all the time.

You go to bed and you think about food. I'm often lying there awake and I'm thinking about food. Maybe we've just done a new menu, but already I know that we're going to have to change it very soon, so I'm wondering what I'm going to change it to. Other people lie in bed trying to get to sleep and they're counting sheep jumping over fences — I'm thinking about new dishes. And you do — you're constantly thinking about it. When you go to bed at one o'clock in the morning, you're thinking about food; you get up at five-fifteen – the alarm goes off and it's time to go to work – you're thinking about food and suppliers. I think any spare moment any head chef's got, any spare moment in his mind, when he's walking down the street or when he's not talking to someone, he's thinking about food.

The job can give you a lot of highs and lows. Each day in the kitchen you never know what to expect. You've got to make it work and keep it together and the best advice I can give is that you take it one day at a time. It's so easy to get carried away with a good day, thinking that tomorrow will be better, and come back in the morning only to find that your ovens have broken down, two chefs have already phoned in sick and the fridges have overheated. This is when things can get difficult, but when it does you've got to show your strength as a manager rather than a chef. It happens quite often and when it rains it definitely pours.

When you get a really big kitchen, with maybe eighty-plus staff, the head chef won't really have to deal with issues like these, he's got the sous chefs (his sergeants) to look after these problems for him. In fact, once he's employed a member of his brigade, he might not even get to see them in his kitchen every day, whereas the sous chef will, and they'll be first contact and listen to everyone else's problems before the so-called 'old man' gets to hear about it. In a smaller restaurant, like mine, obviously the head chef is a lot more 'hands-on', although once again you want to be able to delegate. I've thought about the food, and then I want to pass my thoughts on. I've got a dedicated team and my responsibility is to teach them as much as I can; and when you've done that you need to be able to trust them in the kitchen with their knowledge. Once you can trust the kitchen brigade with your menu, recipes and presentation, then your other job descriptions come into action. Head chefs will be concentrating on suppliers' prices, menu changes, personnel issues, rotas and holiday rotas.

Some heads chefs live a good life around the kitchen and away from home, being treated to lunches or dinners by a favoured supplier, tasty trips to markets as far away as Paris or Italy, and visits to other countries to work with chefs who'll give them ideas for new styles of cuisine that they can bring back and use in their restaurant. All this is obviously paid for by someone else.

Of course, one of the big complaints among chefs is that second-rate chefs are getting top jobs – and they know they're miles better. It's like any other job: the best qualified people don't automatically get to the top. You've got a load of so-called head chefs in the business who'll never get to work in good places because, although they claim to be head chefs, they're not what I'd class as such in that they have no management skills, never change their menus, always use cheap suppliers, have dirty kitchens, never make the budget and can't even cook. These will be the people who probably blag their way to the top and, once they've signed a contract, it's hard for the company to get rid of them. This all means that the dedicated, honest chefs out there who *can* cook miss out on well-paid head chefs' jobs.

Kitchens are stressful. Tempers fray, explode and, as in any hierarchy, the seniors give out the grief, the juniors take it. The theory is that what happens during a busy service is over and done with when that service ends: harsh words, hysteria, potential or even actual blows, all that gets left, as it were, with the KPs for washing up. A new service should be as 'clean' as the pans it uses. But power does corrupt and not all chefs attain this platonic ideal. The ability to cook gets you the job and may well keep you there. But there is more to the job and not everyone makes the grade.

To me a bad head chef is one who walks round all day writing things on the board, pretending he's writing recipes; giving someone a hard time just for the sake of it; telling someone how to do something which isn't right, but he thinks it is; not showing people how to cook; not being in the kitchen when he's most needed; not being helpful; being dirty, or lazy. But, for all that, he can still be a good cook and so he gets away with it. He's probably been like this since he was a sous chef. There are a lot of people in London with head chefs they hate. Probably because they work their nuts off and the head chef doesn't, but if he can cover up when the owners are around he'll be there at management meetings, be there for the Christmas bonus, all that. That's a bad head chef, and a bad head chef is your worst nightmare.

When it comes to managerial skills and respect for other people, the worst head chef I ever had we'll call 'Big Boy'. He knew his food, without a doubt, but running a kitchen he was just a fat, selfish, obnoxious bastard. His man-management skills were shit. He was a nightmare to work with. If they knew 'Big Boy' was on the pass on a busy night, everyone thought, 'Oh fucking hell, no way.' And he'd start sending the food back — just to put people in shit. The staff are doing as well as they can, but they're scared. Every dish they put up has to be spot on. If he doesn't like it, he'll send it back. But sometimes he'd just look at who was on the pass, say, 'Fuck you,' and send the food back: 'Do it again!' Absolute nightmare.

He didn't think anybody should have a social life. My first few months I worked directly under him. One Friday I went in at twelve, supposed to finish at eight. And at eight he said, 'Can you stay for a few more hours?' There was a big party coming in. 'Yeah, no problem.' So I stayed till ten. Then he said, 'We're busier than we expected.' So I had to stay till twelve. He finally let me go at half-past twelve. On the Saturday I was on lunch — but he said, 'Can you come in at ten, finish at six?' 'All right.' I went in at ten a.m. that next day — and finished at one a.m. On the Sunday I was on a middle, started at eleven a.m., finished eleven-thirty p.m. On the Monday I was on a lunch. I was knackered. His attitude was, 'Well, you want to be a chef, don't ya? Can't you handle it?' But I didn't have a choice: if I hadn't done it, he would have really laid into me, made my life hell for weeks. Working long hours every day, getting involved in food and being appreciated by your seniors was one thing; being treated like a gofer was another.

But the thing is he was a good cook. And you had to respect that side of things. So there he was, six foot something, big, still under thirty and head chef at a top restaurant, and he's thinking, 'Well, I can be a bastard if I want to.' And he was. In the pub he'd buy all the drinks. But in the kitchen he'd give someone a hard time all day. He'd have a really bad day with everybody in the kitchen. He'd mess up the pass, send all the food back, really upset people all day. If it was a Friday they'd all finish work and off down the pub and he'd walk in and buy everyone a drink. They got their own back whilst drinking his beer and calling him a twat.

But it isn't just being a bastard that makes a bad head chef. Sometimes it's simply their personal style. I had a head chef once who was really crazy. He had a black book in the office, a handover book for the next day. I read it once at Christmas with my friend, a chef de partie. We were on our own, had loads of good food, drank beer, read this book and laughed and laughed and laughed. It was just full of: 'Re – Tom about blah-blah-blah. Re – Re – Re – Andrew didn't wipe bench down last night.' It was so funny. He was the type to sit in his office all day, come out, give someone a bit of grief, then go back again. In the end he was just a clipboard. If he was on my section, which happened occasionally, he'd say the night before, 'I'll set you up tomorrow on the sauce.' I'd go in the next morning, twelve midday, and he'd have all my sauces out, all my *mise en place* out, all the trays that should have been refreshed. He'd get everything out, reboil it, have it all ready. Trying to impress me. But I'd say, 'No chef, let's put all this back in the fridge, leave this one out, this one out, and if we get busy, I'll put out the others.' 'Oh – up to you!' Get all snotty. But I felt it was up to me to do my own work, to prove myself.

Gordon Ramsay has said, 'You're only as good as your last *crème brûlée*'. I'll never forget that quote. He's right. If we have a good service on Friday night, it doesn't mean we'll be good on Saturday night. It might be lousy. But you can twist it round. I heard one head chef tell this sous chef, 'You're only as good as your last dish – and in this case you're a cunt.' And this lad's standing there, worked there for a whole year – he's burnt himself, cut himself, sweated his nuts off for a year – and this bloke in one minute just puts him down. He gave his notice in the next morning. You don't work for people who say that to you and you just don't say that to people. OK if you're pissed off, fine, but in the end it's still best to try to explain, even if it's for selfish reasons. After all, if you start screaming at someone in the middle of a busy service, they might well walk out. So I always try to make the time to explain, even if we're really busy. And I'll keep my chef in my kitchen for another six months, instead of losing him there and then.

You do get bullying. At Gleneagles that's the way they worked. It was that army thing: they'd break you down to build you up. Everything was, 'Yes chef, no chef, yes chef.' I remember a chef pulling a trolley past the office once with loads of plates on it and he'd forgotten to clingfilm it — usually you'd wrap clingfilm all the way round the trolley to stop the plates from falling off — and it hit a dip and the plates went everywhere. The sous chefs came storming out of their office and went mental at him. In those days they had their own room and you took in their sandwiches and coffee. It was like, 'Yes master, no master.' If someone was messing up, the executive sous would put them in the cold store and shut the door. They'd come out shaking. One day I went to turn a brand-new fresh soup into a big pan. The sous chef above me saw there was a bit of water in the pan: 'That's bloody dirty water, putting soup in there will make it dirty soup. What the ruddy hell are you doing?' But the point is that afterwards he explained why he'd been so angry. And even if I didn't like being bollocked, I understood. Which means when I go to put something in a pan now I always check it first. If that chef had just gone ballistic at me and walked off, I'd have learnt nothing. But he explained why he was mad. Constructive criticism. They can come, put an arm round you and explain, 'We've only done this because we know you've got a good future, blah-blah-blah,' and you realise, 'Wow, they're trying to teach me something here.' Sometimes you take the grief and it's worth it. You learn. That's what I feel about Gleneagles.

When you're head chef everything changes. You have to maintain discipline. And junior chefs definitely mess you around. As far as I'm concerned, unless there's a *real* reason why you can't come into work, just get yourself in here. But someone comes up with a head cold, I mean, a little head cold, forget it.

This bloke told me that, 'Sorry, chef, I feel lousy, I've got a cold.' But I knew he had been out drinking the night before. And next morning he's two hours late coming in: 'I overslept the alarm.' But when we were on our way to a supplier I could smell the beer on him, so I knew he'd been down the pub. So I said casually, 'Go out last night?' 'Oh yeah, went for a few drinks — oh, nothing to do with being late, chef, honest chef, I just slept through the alarm.' I said, 'Fine, you stink of beer anyway. Out on the piss Thursday, come in late Friday and you're only on a lunch and now you can't come in and do a dinner on the Saturday. Yet I'll bet you've done your football training.' A bloke who tries that on — he's got to make up his mind whether he really wants to work for me or not. To have a head cold and try to use it as an excuse . . . And to ring me at five p.m. on a Saturday night when I'm expecting him in, and I've only got three chefs — that's not what I want.

A kitchen's like anywhere else — people fall out, sometimes really badly. You can't expect everyone to get on, but when you're working as a team it can cause serious problems. I had a junior sous chef push me once. I was only a senior chef de partie, but it was totally out of order. He got suspended for it. He was giving the commis chef a hard time, and he was totally wrong — it was him who couldn't handle his job. So I jumped in and told him to cut it out, told him he was rubbish. So he dived at me. I told him, 'Never touch me again,' got on with my job and put in an official complaint about him the next day. He was suspended until it was sorted out. Then he got done for taking a commis chef into the office and smashing his head against the wall. He was sacked. I hated him. Which is another problem for your head chef. If you really hate someone in the kitchen, it's up to him to deal with it. What he should do is to bring you together and say, 'Get on with it. If you can't do that, you leave.' This junior sous chef was so useless at his job on my section in the mornings that when I went in in the afternoons, he'd say, 'All this done, all this done.' I'd say, 'Bollocks, you ain't done that, you ain't done that,' and I'd have a row with him. If I was right, I was right. If I was wrong, I'd keep my mouth shut. I used to dig into him and he'd try and wangle his way out of it. I didn't like him at all. But if you're professional, you work with them, get on with it, just don't talk to them. Last time there was a bit of an argument in my kitchen, it was between two lads who are friends and I thought, 'If they're going to argue and fight they can do it outside.' So I pulled them in and gave them a talking to. I didn't want them in the kitchen like that, they'd just start doing it with everyone else. So you ask them to resolve it, get them transferred somewhere else, or kick 'em out.

When you're head chef you have to know how to manage your brigade. Imagine you're at some big West End restaurant and you're doing 800 covers. You've got someone in front of you who's a complete nightmare. You can do two things. If you stand there and verbally abuse someone in the middle of a busy service to the point where he's not going to take any more, he'll put his stuff down and walk out. All right, you've got thirty chefs in the place, but you'll have to drag someone from somewhere and upset the line, to go and do that job. That stops you for two minutes, but in a kitchen doing 800 covers an hour you just can't stop. And the next day: was it worth it? Or you can just give him grief, but at the same time tell him why you're doing it, what he's doing wrong, how to do it properly.

It's hard to sack someone now. They have to go through three disciplinaries before they get sacked. Quite tough. You're supposed to give them a verbal warning, then a written warning, then a final written warning. It's not like Gleneagles. The head chef there had a commis chef washing pots on Christmas night because he was pissed off with him. The chef didn't think twice about it. If that commis chef had left, he'd have got someone else. If I did that here, yes, my commis chef would leave, but I wouldn't do it. You can't just kick off at people and sack them. My friend sacked a chef in the middle of a Saturday night. He told me, 'I called him a fucking cunt and said, "Get out of my kitchen and never come back and work for me ever again. I don't want to see your face around ever again. I don't want to speak to you, get out of my kitchen!"' – all this because the lad had cut three terrines and they were all different sizes, they weren't exactly how they were supposed to be on the plate, although he'd been a bit annoyed with him over the weeks – and he'd already told him he only had one more chance. So this was the last straw. And my mate just kicked him out of the kitchen, thinking, 'I'm one chef down but I've told him what I think of him.' But I can't do that in my kitchen. It's a professionally run company and I'd be out on my arse. His restaurant is different: it's owned by one person, he hasn't got a personnel department, it's not a limited company.

Let me give you an example of how hard it can be sacking people. A friend of mine had somebody working for him in a restaurant. The bloke had been there for just over eleven weeks, out of his thirteen-week trial period which everyone gets when they start. The problem was he was absolutely useless; he was given lots of opportunities, but he wasted his chances. My friend wasn't satisfied and he decided, after twelve weeks, to say to him: 'Right, this is week twelve. You can stay for your thirteenth week obviously, but that will be your last – I'm giving you a week's notice.' So this lad said fair enough and took it all on board. The lad came in the next day and got changed, got on with his job, but later that day he came up to my friend and told him that if he sees him on the street he'll do him; he'll have to have eyes in the back of his head and make sure he's got someone with him when he leaves the restaurant, 'cos he's gonna kill him, he's going to do him big time. My friend just said, 'Get out now — get your knives and get out now.' So he went, but that kind of thing is scary. You're facing the fact that the lad's got knives, that he might be a lot bigger than you, and you know they could probably give you a good thump.

Kitchen violence has always been there — just look at Orwell's stories about working in Paris — but the truth is that it's probably only come to light because the catering business has got bigger and the media have taken an interest in it. Years ago when you started in a new kitchen it was a privilege to get a job there because, your own qualities aside, the vacancies were minimal. Specialist chefs and good restaurants were far fewer in number. Once you were in these kitchens your mission was obviously to learn as much as possible, however tough it was. There were more college-trained chefs fighting to get into the business and once they came out of their easy college days it was straight into a tough kitchen.

Kitchens can be hard, very hard, and they're not for pansies. Chefs have told me about experiences such as being physically shaken in front of the brigade, held in the air with their feet off the ground; of chefs being scalded with fish irons; or being punched in the middle of a busy service, or bollocked so hard that they cried and did the night's work through fear. I've heard of people having their head held under greasy sink water as a punishment for sending out the wrong dish, or watching the head chef bin a table of six plates of food and making the brigade do every dish again —

the reason being that one of the vegetables on one plate was the wrong size. Of course this put everybody in the shit for the rest of the night, but it didn't stop him then having the audacity to scream at them till the end of service — for being in the shit. And one chef pulled a waiter through the hot pass and punched him in the middle of service. Not one of these boys left the job at the time, though. They tolerated all this and the hardness of their seniors because they wanted to get ahead. That's another side of kitchen experience: total dedication under pressure.

Now there are many more kitchens and you don't have to fight to get into a job, but at the same time too many inexperienced chefs leave when the head chef says, 'Boo!' It's hard work, long hours and almost masochistic dedication. I can assure you that when you talk to chefs who've worked in the so-called 'hard-as-fuck' kitchens, they'll have many a tale to tell. They'll also tell you that they tolerated the hard times because they learned how to cook whilst getting grief — which is the opposite to being given grief and disrespected by a head chef who's a self-made bully but not a cook.

None of the above appears to diminish the enthusiasm with which more and more young people are looking to cooking as a full-time career. Whether or not the present-day touting of the profession as 'the new rock 'n' roll' holds even a grain of truth seems irrelevant. And if it is true, then most junior chefs see the downside: the culinary equivalent of second-rate gigs, rickety transit vans, venal management. Glory is allotted to a talented (and lucky) few. For every superstar there are a dozen wretched commis weeping in the staff washroom after getting on the wrong end of chef's impatience. Pansies, to use the kitchen vernacular, beware.

CHAPTER FOURTEEN
PRESSURE (AND PLEASURE)

For those sitting out in the restaurant, fawned on by waiters, hopefully delighted by what is set before them, their greatest problem the bill that, with the inevitability of death and taxes, brings an end to an evening's indulgence, what happens behind the swinging doors that separate the pass and the kitchen behind it from front of house, is largely unknown. Nor, you might suggest, should it be otherwise. As in a theatre, the front of house reveals the stage, the waiters and customers acting out their predestined roles. We neither see nor need to see backstage, the lighting rig, the dressing rooms, the actors and actresses in roles that would do less than enhance their public image. Were we to do so, in kitchen or theatre, what would be revealed might not be that pretty a sight. The nuts and bolts, the mechanics of kitchen life seem at times something like barely organised chaos. How quality food emerges is both mysterious and even miraculous, a triumph of determination and talent over insanity. Such, you might feel, is the essence of all creativity, culinary or otherwise. And, like any creativity, it carries a price.

Cooking as the new rock and roll? Bullshit. Not the fashion and fun side, anyway. Or the money. It's not rock and roll when you go in to work every Saturday night when your friends are out on the town. It's not rock and roll with the work rotas, the heat, the noise, the unsociable hours, the lousy pay when you're starting out. It's not rock and roll with the amazing pressure which you get in a kitchen. Most of these issues are thrown at you when you start. That's when you decide whether you really want to carry on with it. It's a big thing deciding to become a chef.

At Gleneagles the discipline was driven into you, it was in your head. Do it. No questions. Just do it. And jump. I was serious – but it was because I was so scared. I decided to go to college and learn. I thought: this is never going to happen to me again. The fact I was going to college was a bit of a bonus. They loved it. I was a grafter, I just worked and learnt at the same time. Put my head down and worked. You had to get ready for 300 people every night. There I was, no qualifications, young lad, got to be ready for six o'clock: 220 plates of smoked salmon, sliced and ready in the fridge, ready to go; 120 plates of butterfly prawns.

Seventy-two chefs in one kitchen were frightening. And, whatever they said at school, you are not a pansy. You can walk out of a day in a kitchen like that and say to yourself, 'It's not pansy, being a chef.' A lot of them are really hard people. The kitchen managers kicked your arse. They made sure you were doing what you were supposed to do. They let you know if the head chef was coming round. It was a relief when he was away on holiday. Then it's, 'Chef's back. Help! What are we gonna do?'

The abuse you got when something went wrong was new to me. Once the sous chef said to me; 'Go out and get me a pint of orange juice from the breakfast buffet.' I went to get this orange juice from the restaurant and when I came back there was about 2–3mls missing. Which was wrong: you were told do something, you had to do it. Exactly. So, being all clever, I went to the sink to put a drop of water into it and it was, 'Stig!', which was my nickname – Stig of the Dump, 'What are you *doing* !' He caught me red-handed. I never lived it down. All day he was saying to me, 'I can't trust you, you can't be trusted, you little shit.' Just gave me grief all day. Embarrassing me as much as possible in front of everyone. The sous chefs just think that's funny. And they're saying it while another sous chef's standing there. The sous chef laughs, they all laugh . . . And I was unlucky, got my spots at twenty instead of sixteen. Cue the laughter: 'Caviar face,' 'Give us the crocodile soup and make it snappy,' 'Finish the dot-to-dot on your face before service next time, spotty.' You even felt pressurised if you were genuinely sick. You couldn't be off work – no matter what. One time everyone in the kitchen was having gastritis. I went into work with toilet paper stuck down my trousers because I didn't want to be off work. I twist-ed my ankle one night and went back to my room crying, in agony. The next day I came out of college in between lessons and went to the hospital. They said it was sprained and I had to leave it to rest for two days. I'm not talking about a little sickness prob-lem, I could hardly walk. It didn't make any difference: I had to go back into work because I was too scared to be off work; that's the way they made me feel.

At Gleneagles there were some young boys from Blackpool College, all in their third year, so they knew what catering was about. They were about nineteen or twenty years old. They were thinking, 'Yeah! Gleneagles. Get stuck in to it, we'll do really well here, show 'em how to do it.' One of the biggest, bravest of them broke down one day on the sauce section and cried, stood facing the ovens and cried, because he couldn't handle what was going on. One of the others had to go on the buffet one day, but he was working in the butchery section as well and he got so much grief off the sous chef there to be ready for four o'clock that when he came off the buffet he cried his eyes out because he couldn't get all his work done. Nineteen years old. Just crying his eyes out. One lad had dermatitis like myself and he was a complete wreck. They couldn't sack him; it had been caused by the work, the stress. When he came back to work they had to put him on certain sections so it wouldn't affect the food. So on Christmas Day he was the one the head chef put on the potwash. There were no unions and there still aren't. You put up with it. To overcome the pressure people would get drunk every night because either they couldn't handle it any more or they blamed someone else for their problems. They'd go round beating each other up, loads of fighting in the staff block, though not in the kitchens. People were too scared of the sous chefs. They had to get on with their work, until it was too much. And that's when they left.

There was a pastry chef, really under pressure, and one day he vanished from the kitchen. Someone went to the car park and found him lying on the ground, waving his arms and legs like a dying ant – he'd completely lost the plot. He was off work for about six months. Some people said he made it up to get out of work at a busy time of year, others that he'd just lost it completely, couldn't handle it any more. Even when he came back, he was a bit of a nutter. Very funny man, but a nutter. Then just before the busy Christmas period he twisted his neck or maybe his back – either way he was off work again. So they asked him to leave.

I thought of quitting loads of times. A lot of people did quit because it was too much. If you didn't work hard, you got a bad time. It was scary. You had to make sure you were ready: 440 covers on a busy night. If you got slammed with checks, you had to be ready for it and you had to get that food up. We'd got busy before we knew it and weren't prepared for it. And we got pushed and pushed and pushed. Being shouted at made you cook that food quicker than you'd ever cooked before to get it up on the pass. And I did crack up, once. Just stood there on the pass and cried. I just couldn't handle it. I was being asked to do something I couldn't really handle and I was getting so much shit for it. It was just too much.

Yet, looking back, I know that there was something special about it. The grief I got for a whole year, when it all finished, it was the best thing that ever happened to me. I say that now and I believe it. The senior sous's last words to me were, 'You'll never take this much aggro and grief again in your life. I think you'll make it.' Those words changed me from being a nervous wreck into a competent person in two minutes. But to get to that stage I had to stand in the middle of service and cry because I just didn't know what was going on. I wasn't ashamed of it.

Of course, I didn't know the pressures the chefs above me were under. You didn't have to be at the bottom of the ladder to get pressure. If you were at the top, or near it, there was pressure too, but it was different. I just had the pressure of them giving me grief to get the food out. But they have lots of things to worry about. For instance, if they take someone on who should know what to do and that person can't handle it, they either leave or get trouble all day. But if they take someone on who's not experienced, the pressure's not only on them, it's on the one who should be teaching them, the senior chef who has to train them to do their job. And if that still goes wrong, then the head chef's on to them. The pressure on the senior sous chefs from their boss, the executive head chef, came out in the way they put pressure on the staff below them. When the executive sous chef was under pressure, he would take the head of every section into the backyard with a bin from their section and make them tip the bin out, and if there was anything in there that shouldn't have been chucked out – veg trimmings, old meat, usable salad leaves – they were made to pay. It was a spot-check; you never knew when it was going to happen.

Ten years later, I'm in the position of the chap giving me hell at Gleaneagles. At Quaglino's I was in a position like a sous chef from Gleneagles, thinking I could now give out all the hard times. With the intense pressure of service there, you were always shouting – not at individual people screwing up, but you were shouting for food, pushing people to get it up as quickly as possible. Every night was a headache, your head was pounding because you'd been shouting and shouting all night. Quag's is full of people. When you're busy, you've got everyone on a section, you've got your runners down both sides – they're the tray carriers – they stand by the wall in the front pass and by the wall at the back pass near the potwash, and when the table's away, you shout 'Service' and the runner will pick up the tray you give him and he'll carry it down into the restaurant to section four. Then he gives it to a waiter, who serves it. For every service you've got to be ready, got to be quick, because if not you're gonna sink. And the more you sink the bigger the pressure is to get out of the shit, and then it's easy enough to blame everyone in the kitchen for your errors and that's when you start to shout.

If the sheer pressure, some might term it bullying, is the psychological downside of kitchen work, then there are other pitfalls, and these are more substantial. Drink, drugs, burns, cuts, the ailments that seem to pick on chefs, these too come with the job.

People don't realise the everyday things that happen to chefs. They don't just walk into a kitchen and get on with their work, then go home. Like everywhere else, things go wrong, things happen. It's such a stressful job, people lose concentration, have accidents – nasty burns, cuts, nervous breakdowns.

One head chef I had was a great chef, a really good guy. His only problem was that he used to go into a fridge and talk to the food. He was really stressed, going through a divorce at the time. I'd walk into a fridge and Brian'd be stood there, talking to a pot. Close the door and walk out. Brian used to talk to the stockpots. When he was making sauces he'd stand there with his head over the pot, shaking it, going, 'No . . . no . . .' He'd start a job then walk off. He could make nice food, but he'd forget things. And every night he picked a row with the manager, just for the sake of it: 'I'm the chef, I'll do what I want . . .', that sort of thing. The love of his life was his little Highland terrier, a little Westie. Anything to do with his dog – 'Chef, we'll put your dog in the stockpot tonight' – he'd go mental. It was Brian who put a stop to my tutting problem. I basically tutted at everything that I was asked to do. I don't think I even knew I was doing it, but it drove him mad. One day he went completely mental at me. I've not tutted in a kitchen since. Brian stopped talking to food too.

There was a lad who worked at Quag's when I did. He was very ambitious and worked really really hard. His wife had just had a baby, he was working long hours, not at home much. He wasn't in a senior position, but he was much older than the young ones working around him. And it began to get to him. He had to do all these long hours and they promised him so much – promotion, more time off – but never gave it to him and it was doing his head in. All of a sudden he started going missing from his house, not coming to work. Once he went missing for quite a while and they found he'd cracked up. So he took some time off, got himself back together, came back to the kitchen, everyone thought he was fine, keeping an eye on him. But he wasn't. Apparently since then he's lost the plot completely. He went to work in a big restaurant in London and ended up in and out of hospital for six months, trying to get sorted out. Had to sell his house, lost his job – it all went wrong for him.

Apart from the pressure of working in the kitchen, it's a dangerous place. Under pressure, you start getting annoyed, then you start having rows, lose your concentration. I've seen so many boys pick up a pan and drop boiling oil over their arms. Some of them are determined to carry on, with great burns all over their arms. Of course, the chef should send them home. But many don't. And they make you feel guilty for being off because of burns, so you keep working. You probably get a few physical fights in some places. People will give each other shit in the middle of service for no good reason. Someone lower saying to the person above, 'Fuck off! I ain't listening to you.' 'Don't tell me to fuck off, I'm in charge.' And off they go.

When I was at the Royal Lancaster there was a lad who'd come to work with me on an apprentice scheme, and he was really bright – well, he seemed to be really bright about what he wanted to do and his dad had a lot of money and was going to help him set up a restaurant once he'd learnt his trade. But there was always something about this lad. He had a row with a sous chef and headbutted him; but he survived that. Then, this was after I left, I heard he stabbed one of the waiters because he was winding him up. Then he got sacked and when they searched his locker he had CS gas and all the kitchen knives in there.

There was a recent case of a chef branding someone with a palette knife. This was in a Michelin-starred restaurant. You can

understand the pressure, but still . . . The chef had to go, however brilliant he was. Then there was this newly opened place, a
hotel with several restaurants, where they'd employed a really
top chef, came from a Michelin background. Which should have
been great. What you have to remember, though, is that this isn't
a small country-house hotel with probably one kitchen overloaded with too many staff. This is a hotel with eight different
kitchens and you need about 120 chefs or more to staff them.
So this chef's responsibility now is about running the whole
operation and trusting eight head chefs to lead these kitchens
for him and keep the food to exacting standards. Therefore it's
not just about pretty food any more – it's about management
skills and people skills. Well, this guy obviously didn't have
these skills, to the extent that he even made his head chefs
feel as if they couldn't cook; as for the rest of the staff he simply
suggested they start their careers from scratch, he thought they
were so bad. But this bloke turned out to be the loser in all this:
one night he totally lost control to the point of no return. He
grabbed a young commis chef in a headlock and told him, 'Don't
fuck with me!' Obviously M. Michelin was straight out of the
door – and bang goes what must have been an £80,000 a year
job, plus bonuses. However tough things are, you just can't do
that, and it's nice to see someone paying the price for such
unacceptable behaviour – however great the pressure.

Then there are the medical problems that hit chefs: some
through pressure (nervous breakdowns, insanity), and others
natural: 'chef's arse' (in other words sores that come from
sweat constantly running down one's back. Varicose veins,
caused by the heat, all the standing. Dermatitis. Alcoholism.
Drug abuse. Violent behaviour. Divorce. It's not a sociable job.
You can't have a girlfriend and work doubles every day. You can't

have a relationship unless she works in the trade too. So you go out on a Friday night and just get drunk, have a laugh, have a woman. It's sociable within your own circle. But at six or seven on Sunday night you just stop – you have to get up again Monday morning.

I've got dermatitis, varicose veins, which a lot of chefs get. Varicose veins because you're standing close to the ovens, dermatitis from nerves. I got mine at Gleneagles within three months of starting – I was a complete nervous wreck. I have sorted myself out; if you can take holidays and get away from the kitchen it all calms down, but you still get the dermatitis, you've got it for life. It's this vicious circle: when you touch oils or citrus juices it stings in between your fingers; then because it stings you keep washing your hands, and if you don't dry them properly, that makes the dermatitis worse.

When I first went to the doctor's with my dermatitis, it had got to the stage where I used to rub between my fingers all night and wake up with them covered in blood. So I went to the hospital and they put my hands in this herbal detergent and said, 'Leave it for four or five days.' I went back to work to tell the executive sous chef what was wrong with me and he went ballistic because I was gonna be off work. My hands were covered in scabs and of course I couldn't work. But instead of sympathising he's making me feel guilty about it. So I just said, 'I'll put gloves on and work on another section.' Which he allowed me to do. But I was working in agony. None of the other chefs could believe that I was working in this state. They said, 'Don't do it, don't do it, stay at home.' But I was too scared to have days off. I don't think they'd have sacked me for staying off, but I definitely wasn't about to take the risk of finding out. With a thing like that, they were so short of staff, they'd just think,

'What can we get him to do that won't affect the food? Even if it's peeling potatoes, tying the string on the beef or something.' They weren't happy for you to have any time off at all. They just wanted you to get in there and do things.

You get hernias in kitchens, too, picking up big pans. A boy at Gleneagles picked up a pan one day, boom, had a hernia. Dragged out of the kitchen in agony. You can cut your fingers off, stick knives in your hands. And people can stab you with knives. If you have a row with someone, the knives are there, any one you'd like to choose. A few years back a good friend of mine, working in a top-class kitchen in West London, was stabbed by a commis chef. The boy who stabbed him was off and running as soon as it happened; the police caught up with him and I believe he got three years. As for my mate's head chef, well, he didn't give a toss, and never got involved. My friend had the last laugh, though, this year. We went up to the criminal compensation courts and he picked up a fat wad of money.

Chefs drink. They always have. But it's as much for recreation as for relieving the pressure. When I first came to London it was brilliant. What I liked about working in London was having every other weekend off. There was a Friday morning buzz to get ready, get your *mise en place* done, get through your service, wait for the lads to come in for the dinner shift – 'Here you are then, it's all ready for you, you've got nothing to do, you're all set up' – have a chat for five minutes, have something to eat in the restaurant when the chef wasn't around. At the Royal Lancaster, after two years it got to the stage where we were all eating steak and chips, with beer on ice, before we left for this long weekend. But we knew we were going straight across the road to the pub, which would be just full of chefs who were off that weekend. Even the head chef. And it was brilliant. Always packed out. I used to love it on a Friday night. You'd wake up on Saturday feeling like hell, but you wouldn't care.

At Odette's on a Friday and Saturday before service we'd go into the pub opposite for a beer, then go back to work. There'd be beer in the fridge and we'd just get on with it. We'd drink while doing service, but it gets sweated out while you're working. As long as we ate as well. We'd always eat the espresso tart the pastry chef made. Probably the biggest drug in the world, so strong, full of coffee, double or treble espresso, and that kept you going. We had a great time. We'd do seventy to eighty covers and get on with it. We were in control, knew what we were doing. We weren't running round legless. And it was a buzz. You worked on a Saturday night, then everyone was out at the pub, always out on a Sunday, and you went in on Monday and it was like, 'Oh no, I've got eight sea bass to skin and fillet at eight a.m.' You just wanted to be sick after a whole day on the beer. But you just didn't stop, the adrenalin flowed and it was go-go-go all the time.

There's probably a lot of places now where chefs get drunk all the time and don't really care. But it shows. And while I'd drunk at Odette's, this tiny little restaurant with a very tight, small brigade, when I went to Quag's I stopped that completely. There's just no way you can have a beer before going in to work there. I don't think there was ever a day when I worked at Quag's that I had a beer before I started work. And definitely the same at Soho Soho. A few shandies now and again, watching the England match in the afternoon perhaps. How can you work at somewhere like Quag's, 800 covers on a Saturday night, when you've had a few beers — even two? Too much pressure, not worth the risk.

There are clubs chefs go to. There's a place in Wells Street, Hombre's, and that's just full of restaurant staff — it's a club, open till about four a.m. Massive club. Old-style glitter ball in the middle of the dance floor, three or four bars, even pool tables, loads of scrubbers in there. Even in the eighties it was the classic place to go, everyone loved it. You'd meet everyone involved in the hotel trade, the waitresses, chefs, laundry people, housekeeping staff. Some nights there'd be a lot of army and police in there. The beer was £1 for a half-pint glass. And it was always packed. They've got a place called Samantha's now, just off Regent Street, £7 to get in, and they have nights where it's 25p a drink. A lot of people now go to the Sports Bar, at the bottom of Piccadilly Circus, huge place. When we had a double at Quag's and then off for the weekend, you'd go down the Sports Bar, be there for one o'clock on a Friday night, and it was open till three, get some beers down, just chill out and get pissed with all the people you've been working with, getting grief from, giving grief to. And you get to know people in places like that, so you get to know about jobs too. When the Sports Bar opened, you could take your wage slip to get in. And you can do that in most places now. Some of them look like taxi firms. But you knock on the door, show a little card, go downstairs and they sell canned lager, stay open till six a.m. There's loads of places like that round the West End.

Of course there's drugs in kitchens, without a doubt. The professional magazines have dozens of pieces about it. Speed, whatever. And it's not only for pleasure. Some people are under so much pressure they take drugs to keep going. Believe me, it can get to that stage. Some chefs live a life of drugs and alcohol simply to keep them going even before they get to the top. It's pressure: a cocktail of the basic stress of kitchen work, minimal sleep, physical strain and a desire to be the best. Then you make a dish and watch some critic come in and tear it to pieces. For some chefs that's just too much to take. But drugs are dangerous, not just to your health, but in the effect they have on people – speed makes you violent and there's all these knives about. That's why I don't trust people who take 'em. I've never taken drugs in my life and that's the way it stays. When I was at Quaglino's there were people who took drugs, and that's what kept them going sometimes with the hours they had to work. I'm sure it's worse in places where they go in at half-six in the morning and finish at half-two in the morning.

Maybe I was just young and green, but I didn't realise about the drugs side of it until about 1994. I started hearing then what people were doing. I knew a few chefs who were taking tablets before they went out. Then after Odette's, when I got to a bigger kitchen, a lot of them were doing coke – the ones with top jobs; others were taking pills to keep themselves going at night after working all day. About a year ago a chef got sacked from a brand-new big hotel at a football ground, for making a hash cake for somebody's birthday in the kitchen. Management found out.

I know loads of people who just brag about it – done this, done that. People working for me over the last year, they've come into work looking like shit and you know where they've been, what they've been up to. You see them struggling through the day and their eyes aren't their eyes basically. But they just keep going, go out and have a good time, come back to work, and that's how they live. But if they screw up, they're out. If they say they're not on drugs, it's their word against mine. But you get to know who's on it.

Drink and drugs, violence, mental and physical illness – all these are endemic to the job, but if anything typifies what make a chef's life so tough it's the simple fact of working so long and so hard. The customer may or may not be always right, but they're always there and if last orders are at eleven p.m., then the chefs have to be there to take them – even if there hasn't been a check since ten. Service means just that.

One of the worst things in kitchens is the unsocial hours: you can't live a normal life. Divorce is rife among chefs. It's like the police – the wife has to know what she's marrying into. I'm lucky because my wife understands. First, she's not in the trade, so we don't talk about the job all the time; we don't have to live with it at home. And I can write my own rota and arrange to be off this day or that. But she understands that if I really have to go to work on a particular day, I have to go. It's difficult for a chef to work splits every day then go home and have a social life. I've seen an old chef of mine go through a divorce because of his job. When you were young you had to make the decision of whether or not you wanted to be in the trade and take on the pressure. Now I'm at the stage where the pressures are about doing the right thing to stay in the job and have a family life too.

How many hours does a chef do? Years ago when every shift was a double, it was nothing to be working in a kitchen doing eighty hours a week. When I worked in hotels in Scotland and in Stratford-upon-Avon, a shift *was* a double. You went into work at nine in the morning, had half an hour off in the afternoon and finished at ten o'clock at night. Eleven or twelve hours work a day. Standing up. And if you worked in a place like Odette's, or for a Michelin-starred restaurant, it was even more intensive: you went into work at six-thirty in the morning and you got out of work at one o'clock the next morning. Eighty-hour weeks like I used to work at Quaglino's are nothing. I'm sure you've got a lot of chefs who probably still do that now, who work in a kitchen non-stop day in day out. When we opened the Soho Brewing Company we all worked six and a half days a week for four or five weeks, and we got there at seven o'clock in the morning and everybody got out at eleven o'clock at night. But we did get a bit of a break, because in the middle of the day, after lunch, there just wasn't a lot of work to do because we were waiting, just getting ready for the night time. Trouble was, it didn't mean for most of the lads that they got any real time off. There was no point in going home if you lived fifteen miles away; you might stop work for an hour, but you never actually left the building.

These days, because there's a great shortage of chefs and it's a seller's market, the agencies and the kitchens need to make the job attractive and that means offering you good terms and conditions. So you'll go along and they'll offer you six shifts a week for forty to forty-eight hours; some places will offer you just five shifts a week, which on the basis of an average eight-hour shift is only forty hours. The reality tends to turn out rather differently. A lot of these places that talk about five shifts or even four shifts are actually asking people to work not eight but twelve hours every day. They've signed on thinking it's only forty hours and there they are, maybe working only four days, but putting in forty-eight hours. The reality is that with London chefs being so short-staffed at the moment, everybody will be doing extra hours. The basic system in my kitchen is six shifts a week over five days, so they'll do one double (nine till three-thirty, five till midnight) and four straights (eight till three-thirty or five till midnight). But when chefs are off sick, and that's nearly every day, then someone has to help by putting in extra time. The other thing is simply to do with quality. This isn't a nine-to-five job at any level, but in a top restaurant, somewhere that's got its Michelin stars, or is working hard to get them, the chef is going to have his boys working long, long hours. But in turn they're learning the highest level of the job and, as usual, you know what you're getting into: if you're going to work for a Michelin restaurant or for a high-quality restaurant you know very well there will be long hours.

For some people the pain isn't worth it. A lot of chefs are getting out of regular kitchen work and getting involved with contract caterers, firms who specialise in providing food for companies, or at least their directors. The chefs who are cooking in these businesses are often very good, they've worked in Michelin-starred restaurants, but they don't want to do the hours. Contract catering allows them to cook the same style of food, but instead of working all day long they're in at seven and out at three and that's their working day. Not to mention having every weekend off – which a normal restaurant can never offer. They benefit, but so do the people they cook for: firms whose top people think nothing of spending a hundred pounds when they go out to lunch are now able to stay there in their own building and get the same standard of food served to them as they'd be getting in a Michelin-level restaurant. You can't blame either side and the chefs are probably using their spare time to do a bit of part-time work too, so they are looking at very good money.

In the end, it's up to you: you make that decision when you take a job, so there's no point in complaining, 'Oh my hours are too long.' Tough. When I employ someone I'll say, 'This is what the job's all about, and this is what the hours are,' and if they're still keen I'll say, 'Right, if you want the job the ball's in your court.' It's their decision.

CHAPTER FIFTEEN
FRONT OF HOUSE

Whatever the physical distance from kitchen to restaurant, the passage of food from the 'back room' to the front of house is an abyss. After service, in a moment of relaxation, the chef may choose to work the restaurant, wandering from table to table in search of congratulations, but the reality is that the chef's control of the food stops short when an order crosses the pass. Waiters have no creative input to the cooking of what they serve, but it is the front-of-house staff who are the nearest a diner gets to the kitchen. Chefs put the food on the plate, but the waiting staff take it to the table. They must explain a dish, convey specific demands to the kitchen, bear the brunt of the customers' moods and eccentricities. It is they who can, if such accolades are desired, make the difference between a good restaurant and one that gains its Michelin star. Unsurprisingly the relationship between chefs and waiters is . . . uneasy.

Of course it's easier to get into the business as a waiter than as a chef. A lot of people start off as waiters without any experience whatsoever and then learn on the job. There are a lot of very good French waiters and a lot of very good English waiters, a lot of very good wine waiters, but waiters are often the sort of people who are travelling, or maybe they've come to England just to learn the language, and they'll just work in a restaurant for a few months, they'll get the tips, but they won't be able to do or know a lot about the food. It's just a sort of casual travelling around Europe job.

Front of house we've got a general manager, an assistant general manager, a restaurant manager upstairs and a Rôtisserie manager downstairs; there are supervisors who work with the restaurant managers, and then the restaurant staff itself will range from a *chef de rang* (in charge of a group of waiters) to a commis waiter to a busboy. So as far as a career goes, you can start off as a busboy and go right the way up to restaurant manager.

Taking it from the bottom, the busboy will stand by the kitchen and wait for the trays of food to be ready and when that tray is ready he'll take it to the station. The station is where the waiter will work that day and where he'll have all his bits and pieces: his extra salt and pepper pots, he'll have his sugars, he'll have his dining bills, his extra cutlery, his napkins, his table cleaners. So the busboy will take the food, he'll run the food — you can call him the runner as well — he'll run the food to that waiter on the station he's told to go to and then the waiter will take the food to the table. That's the busboy's job. He's like a commis waiter, a junior waiter, and he or she will run in and out with the food. The waiter brings the dirty stuff back. In smaller restaurants the runner's job can also include taking the food to the table and serving it to the customer. While he's not serving food the busboy will stand at the back, in the kitchen serving area, and he'll polish the cutlery, the plates, cut the bread. He'll make sure there's enough butter, he'll make sure there's enough cups for the coffee. All the time he should be watching what the waiter is doing and learning about the food. And a busboy will probably learn a lot more about the food if he wants to because he's in the kitchen all the time seeing what goes on and how the chef puts the food together; then again they simply may not be interested. It's often just a part-time job.

Waiters get paid by the shift — they get paid a set rate. But most of their money is made up by tips and so on, and a lot of the waiters can actually earn a good deal more money than the kitchen staff — even the busboys can earn more money than the kitchen staff — but what they haven't got is the qualifications a chef's got. But they can get them: a lot of waiters do managerial courses, and again they all just grow in stature as the time goes by. You start as a busboy, you learn, you get to know what you need to learn about the trade and then, if you stay, you can go all the way to the top.

Other staff also work front of house. First, there's the cleaners who come in in the mornings to clean the restaurant before people get there. There's also a receptionist and the supervisors. They manage the waiters, making sure the tables are right, making sure the menus are right, making sure that the *plats du jour* are written out properly. The supervisors will probably be doing recruitment for the restaurant as well, working closely with the chef. The restaurant managers will do all of the administrative work, making sure the cashing up's done properly, again checking that all the menus are the right ones for that day, that the *plats du jour* are the right *plats du jour* and that everything's been typed up properly. They also deal with wine sales: checking what's been sold each night and replacing the stock.

The restaurant manager and the head chef should be on a par, and the information that the head chef feeds to the restaurant manager should then be passed on to the restaurant manager's team. The respect given the restaurant manager by the front-of-house people should be the same as the kitchen staff give their chef and the chef should give his staff. What you're look-ing for is a team that's like the one in the kitchen. Of course, it doesn't always happen that way. People let you down and then, if the restaurant manager's letting you down as well, how can you rely on the rest of the waiting team to be behind you? When things go wrong, it can cause you real hassles. They do things like ask for fifteen tables to be served at the same time instead of spreading them over the whole night's service and that means you're in trouble – trying to get all these tables out, and that's whether there's two people on the table or ten. And if you're making the kind of food that a lot of fine dining restaurants do it's impossible to serve forty-five covers in a matter of four minutes. But the waiters bring in the orders like that and people expect their food to turn up fast and if it doesn't the customer feels it's the chef's fault. They don't know the way things actually work.

I've seen some bad restaurant managers. I remember a situation when the head chef was really ill, so in effect his brigade was 25 per cent down on the team needed for that night. The chef was still in the kitchen; just being there as an extra person reassured the staff that he was there in case it all went wrong, but he couldn't really do a lot of work. On a night like that you'd expect the restaurant manager to slow down the bookings in order to make it a bit easier on the kitchen. In fact, what he decided to do was stuff as many people into the restau-rant as possible – he just filled the restaurant up to capacity, to put the pressure on the kitchen. It was pure bloody-mindedness.

I know restaurant managers or supervisors or trainee managers in companies who've been sacked – thirty-five to forty years old, and they're taking drugs, putting stuff up their nose, and going to nightclubs and they're coming in to work later and later or missing a shift more often than a commis waiter. In a situation like this you think to yourself, 'Can I trust this person to serve the food that I've put my heart and soul into?' How can I work my guts out and then turn the food over to a person who is coked out of his head and couldn't give a damn about what you're doing anyway? For the chef it's very simple; you want the customer to be served the food exactly as it leaves the kitchen, and if the front of house isn't working properly, you're not always guaranteed it will be.

The shortage of waiting staff is as bad as it is with chefs. Again there's only a certain number of London restaurants which are going to grab the brilliant ones. The rest are basically going to have to settle for what's available. You have no choice really but to take what's on offer. So you come to rely on people who've worked in a place for years and who know the place in and out. Now we might have a few who I don't particularly think are up to scratch: in three years' time they might be brilliant, but it's going to take them time to get to that stage.

In our restaurant, it depends how the waiting-on staff are feeling that day. If they're in a good mood, they do well. French waiters can get a reputation for being as arrogant as any waiters in the trade. A lot of waiters live off the fact that they are from a certain part of the world – they're brilliant, you can't do it, they can. Our restaurant's based on a French/Provençal/Mediterranean feel. The restaurant staff downstairs are from here, there, everywhere. Upstairs we've got Polish, French, Spanish and a French restaurant manager. No English. In the end it's a French restaurant, the menu's in French, and French waiters fit the image. But you get good/bad waiters whatever the nationality. Most of the bad ones are the ones that think they're good. That probably goes for chefs too . . .

The standard of waiting-on is part of what gets you a Michelin star. You have to match the quality of the food with the service and there's only a certain number who can fit the bill. In most restaurants you get the food served on to your table and that's it. You go to a Michelin-starred restaurant and the busboy will carry the food out on the tray and the head waiter will be marching behind him; when they get to the table the busboy will stop still and the waiter will take the food up to the guest, put the food down, tell you what your dish is, then go on to explain their dish to the next person, and he'll tell everyone who's dining what the food is that's in front of them, explaining it all in detail. But whether or not you're trying for a Michelin star, you should try to be as professional as possible in the restaurant itself. A lot of places will just take the food up and say, 'Oh, it's steak' and put the steak down. Now this is where you can make or break your reputation with the customer (not to mention get a good or bad review). If you just walk up to the table and say 'Steak' and put the food down, people are not really going to be that impressed. But if you walk up and explain what the dish is and make it sound really nice – basically you talk the dish into the mouth – it makes a big difference. Whether you're looking for stars or not, the more the waiting staff know about the food the better. Knowledge is important for other people too: for instance, a receptionist needs to know how to fill the restaurant, they need to know whether table 105 is going to be free in two and a half hours and whether the people who are going to sit at 105 are regulars and they always like that table.

The chef treats waiting-on staff in a Michelin restaurant almost like a chef out of uniform because they have to pass on the message from the chef to the customer. They will recognise a customer and they will remember him and they will do everything to make sure that the chef knows that he's happy. But only a small amount of restaurants are capable of doing that because they keep the staff all the time, working with their menus day in day out, and they know exactly what's going on. You go to a Michelin-starred restaurant and they're going to have the biggest cheeseboard you've ever seen in your life, and they're going to have the biggest display of breads you've ever seen in your life and so on and so on, and so the waiting staff will have to care and they'll have to put their hearts and souls into it. They'll have to make sure they've got polished shoes, they'll have to make sure that their hair is correctly parted, they'll have to make sure the shirt and tie are right, they'll have to make sure that they walk and speak properly. This is all drilled into them from the start. And on top of that they'll have to know everything about the food they're serving. That should be the case every-where. Whether you're in a Michelin-starred restaurant or not, customers often ask about the food and it's up to the waiter to be able to tell them. Every time we do a new menu we give them an information pack. It gives them a description of every dish, and you then expect them to explain to every customer what that dish is — although that's not as easy as it sounds.

There's no love lost between front and back of house. They both think they're right, but I'm on the side of the chef. The chef can blame his brigade for not cooking the food right, but it has to go past him before it goes into the restaurant. But the head waiter or restaurant manager can't always keep an eye on his waiting-on staff, a lot of whom don't know what's on the menu — that's when chefs get annoyed and take it out on the manager. We give our waiters a description of the food on the menu so they can learn it. A waiter the other day said, 'Where's that yellowy cream we put with the fish soup?' I went mad. 'What do you mean, yellowy cream?' If a critic comes in and says, 'What do you get with the fish soup?' 'Oh, you get a croûton with a — it's like a yellowy cream sauce . . .' 'Sorry, don't think we'll review this place. 'bye.'

Every chef has problems with the restaurant staff. They don't like the chef telling them what to do. They can't handle customers being awkward — a bad customer means a bad night for them. Busy nights always cause friction between head chefs and managers. You can't let it go too far, although in many cases it does.

The relationship between front of house and kitchen stands and falls on whether the front of house take their jobs seriously enough and make the customers feel that in effect they are sitting right in front of the chef. A chef has to rely on them — you can't go out into the restaurant and check every busboy. I think chefs have always got this insecurity about the waiting-on staff, not being absolutely certain the waiter is doing his job properly, especially whether he'll explain the dishes, which the kitchen has put all that work into making. The chef's in at seven o'clock in the morning, he's working his nuts off all day, and when it comes to getting the food out, which is the whole purpose of the job, he expects that waiter to be in work on time, cleanly shaven, shirt ironed or hair tied back or whatever and to be able to serve that food on the table with the heart of the chef, who's been in since the early hours of the morning cooking it all. Now chefs don't believe that the waiters do that and because they don't believe that they have this little hiccup, this little itch, you know — you're not supporting me, you're not doing what I want you to do — and when you feel like that it can get quite ugly. Things irritate you: when it gets really busy, that's when a waiter will drop a plate of food, and when we're quiet he'll take his time with the food and he needs to be pushed to get the food out. And he can mess up the presentation: when the waiter carries the food he'll carry three plates in two hands, he'll tip the plate a bit so the sauce will run, so when you put the sauce on the plate and you think, 'Oh that looks great, it's going to be brilliant. If I was sitting down eating that now I'd be really happy,' what you have to remember is that 50 per cent of the time the plate of food is going to go out and get served with the sauce all over the plate because the waiter is so clumsy. You have to realise that the bus-boys who are taking this food out haven't been in the trade for that long, so they're going to be the worst, but they're still the first person to take the food out. In an ideal world you'd have a head waiter to take the food out every day, but it would cost you a fortune. So, like so many other things, it all comes down to money. That said, sometimes no one, not chefs, not any level of waiter, can defeat pure ignorance. People who just don't, or won't think about what it is they're ordering. What, after all is the point of asking for a dish with roquefort, which is a very rich cheese, and then complaining because it's too rich. Or ordering duck breast, which restaurants always tend to cook rare, and then sending it back because, of course, it's rare.

In the end what we're talking about is trust and some things just make you have this not very trusting feeling about the restaurant staff. About two months ago I had one of my top recruitment agency guys in with an old friend who's also a chef and I decided to send them out an appetiser – a sample of two new dishes that we'd got. And then we sent out the starters and the main courses and a few extra bits and pieces and the dessert. When I was expecting them to be in the middle of the main course they walked in to the kitchen and said, 'Thanks ever so much,' and I'm like well, 'Thank you for what? You haven't even had your main course yet.' They said, 'Oh no, we've eaten, we've eaten.' What had happened is the restaurant staff — again they should know exactly who's on every table — had moved them somewhere else without telling me and our extra little bits and pieces had actually gone to someone else. He was getting all these little bits of food — you know 'compliments of the chef' — and he's thinking, what's going on here? My butcher came in about eight months ago and he booked for eight o'clock. So at six-thirty in comes this table: Hutchinson for two people. Same name as my butcher. I'd told the staff, 'Look after him,' because I was off later I sorted the bill out myself, signed everything, they had their meal and off they went. Then at eight o'clock the butcher came in. The bloke who'd come in at six-thirty had the same name, but the restaurant staff didn't bother to come to me and say, 'Mr Hutchinson's in. Is this the butcher? Is this his name? Is this the right person? He's earlier than expected' and so on — they just let it go. And that's when you lose your trust in people because you trust them to understand or to remember what's what and who's doing what. Or there's the situation when you run out of food, and you say to one of the restaurant staff, 'Can you tell everybody else we've run out of this?' Well, they don't tell everybody and someone comes and orders the food, then you've got to go back to the customer and say, look this is actually off the menu, we didn't realise, and it makes you, as a chef, look very unprofessional. Or you have scenarios when the food gets dropped going out of the kitchen because they're all in a panic. You then have to bring the whole table back and the table are sitting there thinking the kitchen staff are incompetent. Sometimes a waiter will come along and he'll say he's got a new commis and he isn't really up to it. He will drop the food or he will carry the plate as if he's doing an egg and spoon race.

And you have to have a few quiet words with them now and again; they settle themselves down for a couple of weeks and then they get back to the dropping stage and the clumsiness. But the customer knows nothing about this. The customer doesn't realise that a waiter's dropped the food on the floor — or that the reason that they're sitting there getting furious waiting for their food is that the waiter hasn't put the check through yet, so the machine hasn't shown the chef the order and he doesn't even realise there's been someone sitting there for half an hour without a starter.

Of course, that's exactly what the restaurant manager should pick up on, but that doesn't mean they always do. I've been in a restaurant where tables had to wait an hour and a half for their food and I don't understand why the restaurant manager didn't pick up on it. The customers were coming to the pass and saying, 'Where's my food?' If a restaurant manager is any good at their job they should be monitoring who was eating and how long they've been waiting for their food and so on. So this is when arguments start between the kitchen and the waiting staff. Still, it's like arguments inside the kitchen — at the end of the day once the service is finished everyone should be friends again, and usually that's what happens. Everyone has a laugh and a smile about it; so it's not massive, it's not really bad. But as far as the relationship goes, it always depends on the day, it depends on the service — last night was a great service, but is it going to be that good again? It depends on the mood the restaurant staff are in, it depends on the mood the chefs are in. If we're in a bad mood with them or they're not very happy with us that's when it can all go wrong and everybody can start arguing with each other and falling out.

I don't think you could get a chef who'll say, 'No, I never

203

scream and shout.' I know I do, but I hope I don't do it too often, and I definitely don't want to get the reputation for being one of those chefs who gives people shit every day and every night. The job is about getting on with people, but there's also a selfish side: you work for a company and you don't want to get yourself a bad reputation and you don't want to lose your job and you don't want people talking about you and saying how angry these chefs are and how rude and nasty. You try and earn your respect from the restaurant staff, kitchen and front of house.

One of the things that customers never think about is the simple pace of serving. In the way of things people tend to want to eat at the same time — one o'clock for lunch, eight or eight-thirty for dinner — and it makes it harder for the kitchen to cope. Once again, it's different in the very top restaurants. A top chef, with a Michelin star, dictates his own pace. He has the restaurant open from twelve to two-thirty and you've got to go and eat in his restaurant at his time. There might be four tables booked for twelve o'clock, so he won't take the next tables until twelve-thirty. Now if you're there at twelve-fifteen you'll have to wait until twelve-thirty, and if you're there at quarter past twelve and your booking was for twelve o'clock well you'll probably lose your table. His kitchen is obviously under his control, but in this kind of restaurant the customers and the ordering are controlled by him as well because he's the chef, it's his own restaurant, and so on. He's cooking this brilliant food — he gets to say how and when you eat. But most restaurants have to do it differently. You'll find that if you work for a company, then obviously their attitude — which is understandable and it's not being knocked — is that, well, we need to make a certain amount of money every year to keep going so we need all the customers we can get and if they all want to come in at the same time we'll just have to live with that. And one of the ways you deal with that is to say, 'OK, they all want to come in at the same time, in that case we'll just have to make sure we are serving the sort of food that can be served as quickly as possible.' So another of the chef's responsibilities is to work out a menu that suits the pressure of the customers' demands. It makes his life easier and it also means that he has some time to do it properly. If he's not rushed then the standard of cooking is higher. There's obviously some degree of rush – people all wanting food at the same time – but you try to cut it down as much as you can. For instance, at lunchtime you need a menu that you can serve quite quickly; you know you're not going to put a soufflé on for a dessert at lunchtime because people just don't have the time to eat it. Most of them are in some kind of business and they want to be in and out; they don't want to wait fifteen to twenty minutes for a soufflé, however good it is. What you don't do is a dish like one they did at Soho Soho when I first got there. They had a scallop dish for lunchtime on the *à la carte*, and this dish took twelve minutes to cook. (It had pastry round it and that took the time.) Now twelve minutes is a long time when you have people who want to be in at one o'clock and out at two. It just can't be done. Especially if you get busy and you forget to put your scallop in – because you can't speed it up: from the time you put it in it's going to take twelve minutes, and people are waiting for a starter. They don't want to know.

In the evenings, we're open from five-thirty through to eleven-thirty. That's six hours to serve food, and in those six hours we might do twenty-five people every half an hour. That's fifty people an hour, which makes for a lot of customers over the six hours. Even fifteen people every half an hour, that's a lot of customers. But it doesn't work out like that. It builds up and then it fades away. In the average restaurant you'll find that everybody turns up at eight o'clock and the last check comes in at about ten-fifteen, so what's happened between half-five and eight o'clock and what's happened after ten-fifteen till eleven-thirty? People, on the whole, don't want to eat at those times. And in the end it's a business and you've got to do what the customers want. Only a limited number of restaurants can dictate the pace to the customer. In most restaurants the customer will end up dictating it to you because you need the business — you're just scratching your eyes out with the pressure, but if you don't manage you're going to go under. Of course, this is where the receptionist, the person they ring up to book their meal, is very important. If the receptionist doesn't take the bookings correctly and doesn't even try to space it out, but sits everybody at the same time, well then obviously that's something they're getting wrong.

Another problem is when people turn up late for their booking. This happens all the time. There's always a gap between arriving and eating: the twelve-thirty bookings may arrive spot on time, but they're still going to wait until twelve forty-five or one o'clock to actually order their food. And by the time they are ordering, the one o'clock bookings are starting to order as well and you get a logjam. So if people turn up late, it just makes things even more jammed up. People say you shouldn't open a restaurant if you can't cope with this, but it's not about coping with it, it's about trying to set standards. You know what you want to do and if people followed suit it'd be fine. But of course they don't and when all these people come at the same time and the food checks all come in at the same time, and it all gets mained away at the same time — that's when it all gets a bit heated between the front and back of house. I think it's a lot calmer now in kitchens than it used to be. Well, my kitchen's a lot calmer. I think it's because — it's all about disciplinary procedures and the likelihood of people being civil now. The head chef would like to have a lot of control over that, but you have to make sure you don't step over the line. If someone thinks you're rude, they could report you to management, and you don't want that.

CHAPTER SIXTEEN
REVIEWS

A critic, suggested Brendan Behan, is but a eunuch in a harem: he knows how it's done, he's seen it done every day, but he's unable to do it himself. Castration, figurative or otherwise, does not render him (and, since this is figurative, her) dumb. The status of the food critic has risen, as has that of those upon whose creativity he makes his living, over the past twenty years. Not quite household names, such figures as Jonathan Meades or Fay Maschler still wield an influential pen. They may not break restaurants, but it is certain that they can help to make them. How much a chef cares for their effusions is debatable. Everyone likes a stroke, few enjoy the lash. But all criticism is subjective and none more so than that of food. Of all tastes, it must be the most personalised. One man's meat . . . has never been so literal. The confident chef learns to roll with the punches and the plaudits. And anyway, to toss in another quote, this time from Dustin Hoffman: a good review is just another stay of execution.

What makes a restaurant popular? I don't think it's the press, newspaper reviews. If you serve good food in a nice atmosphere and there's a good front-of-house staff who look after people, you'll always be busy. I walk home after a day in the kitchen and think, 'Brilliant, that was really good.' It's a good feeling at the end of a day when you've served a lot of people. You wonder where they've come from – OK, a lot come from concierges, but then why did that concierge recommend us? Or are they here because last week they came for lunch and thought it was really good? We seem to get quite a lot of people from out of London especially on Saturday nights. You've to assume that they've made the journey because they've read a review. They're certainly not passing trade.

I've learnt over the years there's more to life than being stuck in a kitchen and worrying about critics. With reviewers, if they give you a great write-up, fine. And fine too if they give you a bad write-up. If you've got a full restaurant and you get a bad write-up, it doesn't matter. They can write what they like. They don't do the cooking for you. They think they can make or break someone. And some of them can. But it's not the end of the world. I've had about eight reviews in London and they were all good. But I just get on with it. I don't take much interest in reviews at all.

To be truthful, you do care about them and you don't. If you get a bad review, it's easy to say, 'I don't give a shit, I know the food here is good.' When I was in Primrose Hill a well-known chef came in for dinner and no one knew he was doing a review at all. It was my birthday. I'd had a couple of beers in the after-noon, worked that night, rushing around trying to arrange things, meet people. I did the service, and then discovered that he was writing for London's most influential food and drink page. The head chef was off, the owner was away. When the owner found out that I'd done the cooking that night her attitude was, 'I hope it was good. It'd better have been.' So if it's good I'm not in the shit, if it's not good, I am. Bit of a twatty attitude, I thought. In fact the review was very good, and she gave me a £50 bonus. But if the review had been bad, she'd have blamed me for everything, gone ballistic at me. When I walked out of the building I thought, 'Forget it. She's only happy because it was a good write-up.' That's trust for you.

If you get a good review, you're pleased. You've survived. You think, thank God for that. Doesn't have to be a ten-star write-up, just a good one.

I have respect for certain reviewers. Fay Maschler, A.A. Gill, the AA, the *Good Food Guide*, Michelin.

But I don't think food reviews are really about the chef. Like so many other things, it's not what you know, but who you know. Too often the reviewers get too close to the chefs. Which can work two ways. On the one hand they can give kinder reviews to their mates than they should; on the other, because they're genuinely trying to avoid being biased, they don't give some chefs who they might know as friends a review at all; which is equally unfair because these are often really good chefs.

So you don't get too upset about reviews. At the end of the day, they're doing a review about something they themselves don't do – they don't go in a kitchen day in day out and cook, with all the problems of chefs being off, equipment breaking down, whatever. They just write about what they've eaten and that's it. At the same time you know you have to satisfy them if you can because they can try to make or break a restaurant. I've heard that one of the top London critics doesn't get on with my chairman for some reason, apparently because of something he said, so am I ever going to get a good write-up in that paper? If they gave me one or two stars, people who thought nothing of me would think, 'Cor, he's done really well.' But I'll never get that chance because they'll never come in here.

The PR people at Chez Gérard are now just really pushing me and the restaurant. My name's gone on the menu, they're trying to promote me: new chef, new menu. We've had four menu changes in fourteen months and had minimal reviews. We did have Michael Winner in, and that was a strange review. He liked it, but his friends liked it better. I was quite lucky to get a good review from him. I bought the paper and read the review and thought, 'Thank God for that.' You may not care about reviews for yourself, but if your friends see it . . . The first thing a chef thinks about is who knows him and who'll read the review. When you're actually working in the kitchen you soon realise how little reviews actually count. Word of mouth, on the other hand, is really helpful. For instance, we'd expected to be quiet after last Christmas, but in fact we were packed. But we'd had no write-ups at all. It's just people realising we're doing really well, a lot of people talking about what we do. Last time we had a write-up, it was in the *Independent* magazine and didn't make any difference to the customers we had in. It probably does give customers confidence to go to a place. In any case, even if you get a good write-up, and everyone turns up the next night, it doesn't mean they'll get the food that was written about. You might be especially busy with very few staff. The service goes differently every night anyway. To guarantee perfect food in a perfect restaurant, in our place, we'd all have to do doubles. If I had myself, one on sauce, one on fish and one on larder, and we worked five days a week, doubles every day, that's where you get your standards. If we had that, what a reviewer wrote about us on a Monday would be the same as on a Friday. That's what was good at Odette's – it was a little team and we all knew what was going on and we could all cook it.

In the end the trouble with most reviewers is that they forget what they're there for and spend too much time telling you how clever they are. From the chef's point of view, and I believe from the customers' too, the only thing we want to know about is the food. If reviewers write honestly, 'I ate some chicken, it was dry, over-cooked, burnt on the top, tasted like cardboard, I'll give it a two,' well that's fair enough. But what we should all remember is that everybody who eats in a restaurant is a reviewer and a critic. They just don't write it down.

POSTSCRIPT

The interviews that constitute the bulk of this book took place in 1999 and 2000, when Andrew Parkinson was head chef of the Groupe Chez Gerard 'signature' restaurant Soho Soho. Then early in 2001, things changed. In the first place the directors had decided that Soho Soho, if not venerable by restaurant standards, but with sixteen years' trading behind it certainly mature, needed a thorough overhaul to bring it into line with the newer style of design and layout seen in its local peers. Still popular, it was seen as 'old-fashioned' in relation to its rivals, who promote and profit from 'wet-sales' (i.e. their integral bars) as much as they do from the sale of traditional meals. It shut down at the end of March, reopening nine weeks later, after an £800,000 overhaul that saw the removal of the downstairs rôtisserie, a substantial new bar upstairs, and with the 'fine-dining restaurant' resited and refurbished on the ground floor. The kitchen remains where it was, but has undergone major renovation. Staff have been cut from 60 to 44. What also went was the name: the Group owns the name Bertorelli's (a much-loved Italian family restaurant on Charlotte Street, part of that area to the north of Oxford Street known as Fitzrovia) and, in its abbreviated form Bertorelli, it has become their third brand-name, joining Chez Gerard itself and Livebait. Thus Soho Soho vanished, to be rechristened Bertorelli Soho. This will be Soho Soho's third incarnation. Like a number of other GCG sites, it had been a bank before it started life in the late eighties as a culinary 'recession-buster', serving rôtisserie food only, with all-inclusive covers of ten pounds maximum. The nineties saw success and expansion: the fine-dining upstairs restaurant was added on, along with its attendant private room. The latter will continue but the original 'fast-food' cooking of the rôtisserie will not return. And as Bertorelli Soho the old Mediterranean/Provençal menu has been abandoned: the new food is 'Italian', a change that is not merely in tune with the name, but with what GCG see as Soho's dominant demographic: 25—45 year olds, predominantly female, with disposable incomes and a liking for what is seen as healthy Italian, rather than supposedly rich French food.

What the new restaurant also lacks is Chef Parkinson. At one stage it had been suggested that he should stay on and open it. In the event, as is the custom among GCG chefs, he has moved within the company, taking over the kitchen at the substantially larger Bertorelli Charlotte Street, founded in 1913 and the original of a number of Bertorelli's (in Floral Street, Covent Garden and, both long-since closed, in Queensway, West London and on Shepherd's Bush Green). Bertorelli's is one of the veterans of Charlotte Street's restaurant strip: older Londoners will remember such establishments as the White Tower, Schmidt's and the many Greek restaurants once on offer. Not to mention the original Chez Gerard itself, once an independent 'French' restaurant. Today the old names may have gone but Charlotte Street is as restaurant-heavy as Soho itself. Among the many establishments on offer are Elena's L'Etoile (home of one of London's best-loved culinary chatelaines), the Michelin-starred Pied à Terre, Rasa, a sophisticated South Indian fish restaurant (itself part of a 'mini-chain'), the veteran Greek Anemos, and many more. Five years ago GCG bought Bertorelli's, dropped the apostrophe s and totally renovated the old place. The old Fitzrovians of 'Berts'' heyday — the likes of Anthony Powell, Dylan Thomas, Julian Maclaren Ross — might not recognise it, but they'd probably give it a try. Like Scott's Brasserie San

Quentin, and its newly refurbished Soho 'cousin', it is one of the group's most important concerns. For its new chef, it is a challenge, a chance to put experience into practice and, as ever, an opportunity to learn.

What happened last December (2000) was that the company decided to redevelop Soho Soho. Basically it was a matter of age and style: it was about sixteen years old and while it had had a long period of success it wasn't doing as well as it should have been doing, mainly due to the number of restaurants that had opened in the area over the past few years, restaurants that were building up a new style of service, especially by offering not just food but the sort of spacious, comfortable bars that have become very fashionable and very popular. The original plan was a simple revamp, keeping the name and just doing up the restaurant, but in the event they decided that the change had to be more fundamental. It's a great site, right in the middle of Soho, but the reality was that it needed more than a simple facelift.

What they came up with was taking the Bertorelli brand name that they already had over in Charlotte Street and making a new restaurant in the Soho shell: Bertorelli Soho. For a time they considered opening it under one of their other brand-names, either as a Livebait restaurant, specialising in fish, or as another Chez Gerard, with the traditional French style. They even considered having them both: Livebait upstairs and Chez Gerard downstairs. But neither plan seemed right, and they decided to make it the third Bertorelli after Charlotte Street and Floral Street. The plan is that if this goes well, they can create a whole range of Bertorellis, in and out of London.

Of course age doesn't always mean you have to do a complete change. Look at somewhere like the Ivy – it's been around for ever and just goes from strength to strength – but in fairness, Soho Soho, however popular it is, isn't that sort of place. It doesn't have that celebrity status. So there was no guarantee that a revamp by itself would be enough. The fact is that profits were slipping. With somewhere like the Ivy, it's different: they're making lots of money on the business, they can shut down, have a revamp and when they reopen, they'll make even more. But at Soho Soho that couldn't be guaranteed. I think they'd have been wanting to make the change some time ago, but there hadn't been the proper opportunity. Now there was, and that's what they decided to do. So for the Group the fact that they've got two Bertorellis already operating that do really well, made it seem logical to drop Soho Soho completely and relaunch the site as a completely new place.

This is the way it is in restaurants now, especially when the place is part of a group. You have to keep going forward. So Soho Soho is changing. And it'll change again one day. If in five years or ten years or whenever it's starting to fall behind again, and if the profits are dropping off, then the builders and the designers will be back.

What happens now is that they'll shut it down completely, cover it with scaffolding and rags and whatnot. They'll rip pretty much everything out and start from scratch. At the moment it's got a ground floor rôtisserie and kitchen, which is open-plan so that everyone can see the food being cooked on the spit roast and so on, plus a downstairs bar area where people can sit, as well as a service bar that serves the drinks for the rôtisserie. That's all going to go completely. In its place is going to be a 140-seat restaurant. At the moment the restaurant upstairs can seat sixty-seven and has no bar area whatsoever, just a dispense bar hidden behind a wine cupboard store. They're going to knock that out completely and turn it into a modern lounge bar. Today, that's what people want. It's a good room, it's on the first floor so it's high up, it's got a good view of the street. You can sit around in luxury overlooking the street. The old wine store and dispense bar will go and in their place will be a long bar for serving customers, either at the bar itself or at tables.

The private room stays, although instead of people having to walk past the kitchen, they're going to put in a proper, separate entrance. The room itself won't be changed, although they're thinking of putting a divider in to separate it into two parties, or one dining party and a drinks party, or whatever is needed on a given night.

As far as the kitchen itself is concerned, there'll just be the one, which will stay where it is, on the first floor. There'll obviously be new equipment (though the usable old stuff will stay), but the layout is going to be altered too. At the moment the pass gives out onto the short corridor connecting to the upstairs restaurant. Since that restaurant has gone, that layout wouldn't work. Instead the kitchen will be redesigned: the easiest way to describe it is to say that everything will be moved 45 degrees. So that instead of facing through the pass and onto that corridor, it will now face the wall on which the pastry and larder section are sited. The old pass will be blocked up so anyone walking along the corridor won't see the kitchen at all. With the new restaurant being downstairs – and the single kitchen being on the first floor – they intend to put in a shaft system – three lifts – with serving hatches for the food to go up and down. And on top of this they have the usual stoves, prep tables, fridges and of course the plate and pot wash areas.

The pass will be close to the dumb waiters. The chef will plate up the food, put it on the pass and it will then be transferred to the dumb waiter. There's two shelves in a lift so if there's a big table everything for that table will go down by itself, and if there's two small tables, you can do two tables at a time. It'll all go down on a tray with lids on and the check will go down with it to say which table it's for. There's a possibility they might put a plate wash downstairs so they don't have to keep sending dirty plates upstairs. The same chef will operate the lift and the pass. Instead of being on the cooking side of the kitchen, plating the food with the kitchen staff, he'll be on the other side — opposite them and near the dumb waiters. It will be his job to arrange the plates and trays and make sure it goes to the right table.

None of which, other than as a matter of personal interest, really matters to Andrew. He left Soho Soho in early February and set out to tackle the new phase of his professional life. That Bertorelli's had a ninety-year history is pretty much irrelevant — even if one waiter can boast a fifty-two year record of service, and some of the older chefs have been working there for more than twenty years. For him it is a new restaurant, he is the boss, and his first tasks are to make that clear, both in practical terms — arranging the kitchen and its workings on lines that he sets down — and personally, in his relations with his new team.

Originally the plan was that I'd stay at Soho Soho, waiting for the revamp and then relaunching it as Bertorelli. The management came to me with the plans for Bertorelli Soho, explained what they wanted to do and asked me whether I wanted to do this or not. And I thought, yes I do. There was going to be one big change — because it was going to be a Bertorelli, I would have to start cooking Italian food, and no more French food or modern

British. That didn't matter. At the end of the day, I felt that if I could produce good food and we have a full restaurant and I enjoy my job and I've got a great team of chefs with me who like working with me and want to make it successful, well it'll be the same as working in a French restaurant. I was thinking that it would be a challenge, and I was looking forward to it, but it never happened. One day, out of the blue, they asked if I'd like to move. They thought I'd be a bit shocked — you know, leaving Soho when I was just about to get a new kitchen and a new restaurant — and at first I guess I was, but after a few days I got excited at the idea of moving. It was a bigger place, and while they understood that there was always a chance that I wouldn't like it, they felt that if I did like it, I'd really really like it a great deal. I'd been at Soho Soho for over two years and I was thinking about leaving anyway, and not necessarily moving into another GCG place, and they wanted to keep me. So I took the job. It's in the same company, a lot of things are the same, but I've still got a challenge from day one: OK, you did well at Soho Soho, and now you're in the Bertorelli at Charlotte Street, what can you do here? Yes, it's a bit of gamble: it's like taking a boy who's worked on the grill for two years and he's really good at it — and putting him on the fish; there's no promise that he'll be able to do the fish. So they put me into Charlotte Street Bertorelli, knowing or hoping that I can do the job. But they trust me, and I've proved myself at Soho Soho. So they're not gambling that much.

My new restaurant is a much bigger place. Downstairs there is a big, long bar, with a certain number of tables for eating. Upstairs there's another big room, with two side rooms which can either be partitioned off for private parties or integrated into the main restaurant area. All in all there's about one hundred covers downstairs and room for another eighty on the first floor. It's a bit like Soho Soho in that the downstairs food (like the old rôtisserie) is simpler – mainly pizzas and pastas – and the 'fine dining' *à la carte* stuff is kept for upstairs. But the real difference is the kitchen itself. Instead of one space on the first floor tucked away between the salon and the private room, it's in the basement and takes up an area equivalent to the whole of the ground floor above it. It's essentially a square, with internal back stairs for the waiters to go up and down, and service steps leading straight out to Charlotte Street for taking deliveries, putting out the rubbish and so on. In this area I've got an office, I've got a dry store bigger than my last rôtisserie kitchen, there's a triple size walk-in fridge, and immediately outside and running along its external wall is a large pastry section. There's a massive washing up area, a room to itself, which has also got a convector oven and a low gas burner for the stockpot and a solid top for anything that needs to be cooked at the back of the kitchen. This is very useful when you're doing a private party – the chefs can get on with the party cooking there and they don't have to interfere with the rest of the kitchen. This back area alone is bigger than most kitchens I've worked in: it's got a long pot wash area, a plate wash area, a large table on which the waiters leave the dirty plates and cutlery. It's tiled, like all kitchens, only this time the tiles are white instead of the brown at Soho Soho. They're also in better nick; I presume it was all redone when they took the place over.

In the main part of the kitchen there are two back-to-back ranges. There are three solid tops, two fryers, one charcoal grill – three feet by two feet – and three bain-maries. Two of these are rapid-boiling high-temperature bain-maries (or rapid-boiling brat pans) which are used for cooking pasta. In a section on its own, with a marble top, there's a pizza oven – it's massive, absolutely huge. It cost £12,000. If you order a pizza it can be rolled and put in the oven and cooked and out in four minutes – which is absolutely fantastic. There's a huge hot plate. As well as all this there's a shower room, although it doesn't look as if it's been used for years and seems to be mainly a storeroom for odds and sods, a 'dungeon' under the street where the chemicals are stored, a lift that takes garbage up to the street and brings down deliveries, and a boiler room in which all the staff can put their bikes and hang their washing in if they get wet on the way to work. So all in all it's a big spacious kitchen.

While it's only one kitchen, as opposed to the two I had at Soho Soho, the brigade is bigger. There are lots of chefs scurrying around getting ready for the service and then when it comes to the service there's one chef doing the fish, one doing the grill, one doing the pass, one doing the pasta, one doing the starters, one doing the pastry, one doing the pizzas. You probably also have two chefs to help out when you get really busy. So you're looking at about eight chefs in a service, double what I used to have.

So what I'm looking at isn't a completely different kitchen, but one on a different scale. There's not really any more administration than there was at Soho Soho. I just have to get it up and running in the way that I like it – and the way that I've learned from my other kitchens works best. Basic admin is vital, though: I've learnt how important it is to walk into an office in a kitchen on your first day and to make sure all your files are in order and your records are up to date and sorted. Then you get the rotas worked out, check the ordering sheets, the stock sheets, the *mise-en-place* sheets, get rid of any information that's been there for a long time and which you won't be needing – and all in all have everything up and running in the office before you even get into the kitchen. There are a few different things; for instance we make our own pasta here and our own bread – both of which we used to buy in – and of course the fact that we have more covers means that there's more food to get ready. All of this I have to come to terms with. But as I say, it's scale: just a little bit more fish when you do the fish prep and a little bit more meat when you do the meat prep. That's it – it's just a bigger kitchen with lots more chefs.

I still have no intention of turning into a hands-off clipboard chef. Once I've got the place running properly, I intend to get back into the kitchen, back into cooking. Just because you've got plenty of chefs it doesn't give you the excuse not to work in the kitchen yourself. All right, more staff means you've got more people to watch and more things to sort out, but that makes it even more important than you're not stuck away in your office. You need to be in that kitchen to make sure that they're all doing the grill right, or the fish, or the starters.

On my very first day there I took a good look at the set-up and at the people working there. I knew that I would want to make changes, to get things running the way I like them. I started with the ordering systems, all the staff personal information, then the suppliers and the maintenance of the kitchen equipment. I got an electrician in to check the kitchen – the plugs on the blenders, the wall sockets, any lights that aren't fitted properly, loose wires on the fridges. The fridge company came to check the fridges, and a maintenance company to check the stoves. I used the same company we had at Soho Soho, and we decided to move all the cookers and stoves around and put them in a different order, putting the ones that we'll use most in the main area and moving the ones that aren't very useful to the back area. I also did a general clean-up.

Next I introduced the sort of working practices I want. When I went in on that first day I noticed there were no *mise-en-place* sheets on any of the sections to tell them what they needed in the fridges ready for 12 o'clock service. I spent the next weekend drawing up the sheets and they were ready for Monday morning.

I sharpened up the records of fridge temperatures and changed the way the general kitchen paperwork gets done. When I arrived it was the responsibility of the general manager, but I've changed that. I like to see the invoices, to know how much we've spent, how much we've made.

As far as the actual cooking is concerned, the big thing is obviously that I've gone from cooking Mediterranean/Provençal style food to cooking Italian style. How do you do it? Basically you use your experience and teach yourself. Instead of going out and buying French cookbooks, which is what I did when I put together the first menu at Soho Soho, you go out and buy Italian cookbooks and see how that's done. I'm not saying you simply write Italian recipes straight from the cookbooks, but you use the books to give you an idea of what the main ingredients are, how to use the garnish properly; for instance if you are going to put basil in a dish are you going to put basil in with, say, asparagus – and the answer is that, no, you don't do basil with asparagus you do basil with tomato, and that's the sort of thing you pick up. For instance, they don't use a lot of butter sauces in Italian cooking. Also there's the style of serving: the Italians serve the food in what I'd call quite a 'rustic' way. Not like the French who serve it like real 'Michelin' – all nicely tightly packed. I'm not saying Italian food is just thrown together, but it's not served with the finest attention to detail you've ever seen. The food may be amazing but they don't have haute cuisine

223

in Italy. So you check the books and eat in a few Italian restaurants and that way you get to know what they cook and how they serve it and just by doing that it gives you a few ideas and then basically you start playing about with it. At the end of the day it's not so very different, nothing that is going to blow your mind, but it's Italian and not French and that's the way you go. So, for example, you wouldn't use a pork and leek sausage when you could use a *cottecino* – a sort of Italian sausage. Makes it all authentic. Again, the ingredients are different, but you still buy all your fruit and vegetables from Covent Garden; you probably buy a different type of meat for the Italian sausages – probably different cuts of meat. In the same way, it all comes from the same places; you probably do get a few specialist suppliers – after all they get the good stuff and know about Italian food – but if you didn't use them you could use suppliers you'd been using all the time and they'd go and get the same stuff for you. It's really a matter of reading it and playing with it and making it right. And looking at other restaurants, looking at other menus, looking at books, and that's how you build yourself around it.

What I also do is keep a notebook in which I can put down stuff – recipes, ingredients – that I ought to use. Every day I'm having a little wonder and I'm planning what can I put on the menu and I'm looking at things and already I'm thinking, here's something I can do. I've put together a list of ingredients, main ingredients, that I've found through a good Italian book: there's the herbs they use, basil, oregano, rosemary, parsley and sage, there's always fennel, aubergine, courgettes, red and yellow peppers, plum tomatoes, swiss chard, cavallo nero, rocket, tomato pesto, basil pesto, garlic, pancetta, prosciuttos, cured sausages like salamis, carpaccios, risottos, mozzarella, sardines, anchovies, lots of pulses, pecorino, artichokes, polenta, balsamics, rabbits, liver, porchetta – the pig that I used to do downstairs in Soho Soho is a porchetta, an Italian-style pig, I'll suggest that for the menu because I know that we're going to do really well with it.

One thing I had to do is meet my suppliers. With me starting, all the suppliers were ringing me trying to get a piece of the action. They find out and ring you up straight away. I had a bloke from Bermondsey, trying to sell me all his Italian imports. I didn't want to know. He was doing chickens, but I have that sorted anyway, and all these jars of pesto. But I told him: my chefs won't learn anything if they start getting their pesto ready-made. In the end I'll stick with the people I know. I'll invite Chef's Connection down, show them the place, talk to them about it, talk to them about prices again – and if then I feel that they can do the job for me instead of the company we're using at the moment, then I will. The fish suppliers that are in place I've used anyway, I use them all the time, so they're fine. The meat people are also the same, but I have had to organise how they prepare our meat, because at the moment there's no specs on line. They just buy six pounds of fish and five pounds of filet and so on. I'll be changing that. Telling them exactly what I'll be wanting.

At the beginning I'm as much 'on probation' as anyone starting in a new kitchen. I think the Group know what I'm capable of but they're obviously going to be keeping an eye on me till I find my feet. They want to make sure that I keep in line with what I'm really supposed to be doing, that I don't sidetrack into oriental dishes or something crazy. Because if you're new to the Italian restaurant style and the Italian food style, there is quite a lot of pressure to make sure you do do what is right and it is quite easy to go astray and all of a sudden put a dish on that's British or some other cuisine, not even Italian at all. The truth is that when I arrived the menu wasn't as 'Italian' as you might expect. There's the staples, stuff you'd automatically get in an Italian restaurant, but that doesn't cover everything. So I'd like to change some dishes because there's no 'Italian' in them whatsoever. Which is all wrong: if somebody walked in and said, well there's not one bit of Italian in the actual depth of the menu and actually I don't really like it, I'd be a bit embarrassed. OK, I'm not Italian, but I'd rather be proud of working in a restaurant that's supposed to be Italian and having people say, it's got nice dishes, it's got a nice menu on, maybe it's not completely Italian but the Italian touches are there. I'd be happy with that.

Because the restaurant is a Bertorelli, as opposed, say, to a Chez Gerard, and because the cooking is Italian, we do have certain dishes, brand dishes as you might say, that have to be there. Things like veal Milanese, spaghetti carbonara, spaghetti bolognese. The classic Italian stuff that everyone expects. All in all there's about five dishes like that that are on the menu on Bertorelli Floral Street and Bertorelli Charlotte Street and will presumably be available in Soho when that opens up. Obviously we have to stick to the brand dishes, but we can also do our own Italian-style menu to create a bit of individuality. Each Bertorelli restaurant is in a different area, and has slightly different people coming in – for instance Charlotte Street is a very media/PR sort of place – and one kitchen might have specific facilities to do particular dishes, while another is better suited to different food. The other thing, which I suppose is more 'political', is that if every Bertorelli is doing the same menu, chefs might well argue over who is doing things 'right'. If people are doing their own stuff too, you're going to avoid all that. The main thing is that the 'ops' director knows and agrees before you put anything new on the menu.

One new thing for me is serving pizza and pasta. Some of the pasta, the stuff without fillings, we'll be buying in. A good pasta supplier is now as important to me as a butcher or a fishmonger. I want to know that if I buy tagliatelle it will have been freshly made that day, and if I can use him and save money (and pay my chefs better money) because he's bringing that in for me, well I'll do that. So we'll do that with the tagliatelles and the linguines and the spaghettis and so on but when it comes to making raviolis and tortellinis and cannelonis – the filled pastas – that's where we can make our own and that's good for the chefs in the kitchen who don't know how to make pasta and can start learning. So there's some things that we will do and some things that we might be able to save time by getting them in – buying in fresh. Good pasta sales make good profits.

Pizzas are another great money maker and we have a fantastic oven to make pizzas with. The base is always the same and then it's a matter of what you're going to put on top. So one week I might want to put an olive and asparagus pizza on the menu, another an olive and artichoke pizza; when you're changing the menu, one of the easiest things to do is change the pizza toppings. In the same way, when you do a special – which we do every day – you can do a different type of pizza using things you need to use up. It's all very economical.

At Charlotte Street we've got a café as well as a great restaurant above it. Everything comes out of the same kitchen and they're both very busy. So when I write the menu I need to ensure that whatever we do upstairs can be served downstairs as well; we'll probably charge a little bit less downstairs, but really you've got to do the same dish in a way – but then it's all about the surroundings and people will have the choice of the two restaurants when booking.

The first few weeks have been a transitional period. The old head chef is going off to Riyadh, but we're overlapping for a few weeks. That could be difficult — competing egos and all that — but in fact it's fine. I already knew him because I know the restaurant as part of the group, so when I got the job I asked him about the good and bad points of the kitchen. We had a good chat and he told me how it was and about the people and everything. He doesn't want to get in my way and I don't want to step on his toes, so I have to let him see that I'm changing things so that they'll suit me and not because I didn't think they were any good. He was a bit gutted by some of the things I did when I got there because he felt it reflected on him — but now he's said to me that he's going to take some of the ideas that I've put into place in the office and in the kitchen — and going to use them when he goes to Riyadh. Which is great for me because he could have just got pissed off with me — he could have rung in sick for three weeks. So I'm quite pleased with it.

The other person I had to talk to was the senior sous, who had probably hoped to be promoted when the old chef left. In the event he wasn't, and I think that originally he was very pissed off about the situation. So my job when I first met him was to sit down in the office before we even worked in the kitchen together and just ask him straight out: 'You didn't get the job, how do you feel? How's it going to affect working here with me? Are you going to leave and if you're not going to leave and you're going to stay, why do you think you didn't get the job and what can we do about it? And obviously if you don't want to stay and work for me, well then the quicker you go the better.' His reaction was, no I want to stay, I'd like to stay, I'd like to see how it goes. So now he's got to prove to me that he means it, and at the same time I've got to prove to him that I can guide him into doing things that he's never done before, because he may have been thinking, oh head chefs don't do that or sous chefs don't do that. My responsibility is to make him do these things because I know he'll learn from it; his responsibility is to look at the things I'm pointing out to him and to think to himself, well maybe that's why I didn't get the head chef job and if I do do it this way instead of that way maybe I've got a better chance next time.

This is a much bigger brigade than I've had before. I've got a senior sous, a junior sous, and a tournant, as well as the usual chefs de partie and commis. They do six shifts a week, which is the basis on which most restaurants employ staff now. So as long as I stay on budget, it's obviously up to me how I use my wages and how I pay people. Also who the people are I have working here. Because at the end of the day I need the confidence – if I'm on the pass at the front of the kitchen waiting for the food to come towards me to send to the restaurant I need to be confident that the people behind me on the sections are strong enough to do the job I want. If anything I've got too many people – at the moment I think I've got four more staff than I need. So if I can lose those four people and save that amount of money I will be able to pay the remaining chefs a better wage. I'll be paying them a better wage for their commitment: yes, their wage packet will be fatter but they will have to work for it and if they don't – they'll just have to go. At the same time it means that if I do want to bring someone in, I'll be able to offer a better wage than they're getting at the moment. Eight strong people are better than twelve average people and I'd rather pay eight strong people good money than twelve average chefs shite money.

The restaurant was doing fine when I arrived, but the quality of some of the chefs, the way they worked, the cleanliness, everything they were doing — I just wasn't satisfied — and that worried me. I'm not someone who's going to go in and say, 'I don't want you here, go and work somewhere else'. I'm a person who can walk in and say, 'I can see what skills you have got, but I think you could use them a bit better. Why don't you try this?' So they start to listen to me and think, 'Oh he's all right you know, he's trying to help me, he's not coming in banging away trying to get rid of people'. I have to prove myself to them and make them want to work for me.

Of course they do watch me; I'm their new boss. At the same time I have to watch them, because that's my job. So they get more worried than me, because they're thinking, 'Oh my god is he looking at me thinking he's going to get rid of me?' And I get worried as well because when I look at the quality it isn't always there. It's a good challenge though, to improve their skills and promote them.

In the last two years, people skills is one of the biggest things I've learnt. Management skills. At one time, if someone was having a bad day or was crap and had only been there for a few days, I would have walked in and just said get out. Now it's a matter of trying to talk, to explain, to be positive instead of critical, however much they might deserve it. I want to improve their performance and try to make them realise that if they're going to be a chef, and they want to be in this trade for a long time, then they've got to start from scratch. They've got to start getting it right now rather than saying, 'Ah well I'm only young.' So I've learnt how to deal with people as well.

I'm bringing another sous chef and Andreas, my pastry chef from Soho Soho with me. The pastry chef is well known as probably the best pastry chef in the company and I was lucky to have him at Soho Soho and I'm very lucky indeed to have him come along with me, where I can offer him a much bigger kitchen. And now he can take that further; he'll also work with the desserts at Floral Street Bertorelli. He will spend three days at one place, one at another and one at the other. At Bertorelli Soho, they'll probably have their own pastry chef, but Andreas will be keeping an eye on him or her, making sure that they are sticking to recipes and helping if anything's wrong. Like a pastry doctor if you want, he'll be there. He'll probably have to do more work at Floral Street than he will at Soho — they haven't made their own desserts there before now — but his main base is Bertorelli in Charlotte Street. This will lead to a great standard of desserts (and hopefully bread) in all three Bertorellis.

They're both keen to make the switch but not immediately. I don't think it's right to go in there straight away with a new team, because I think that scares the old team and they start to panic. It's definitely easier to take someone in there after you've found your feet. You can find out the strengths and weaknesses of the team you've got at the time, and then when they come you can talk to the new people about it and they know what to expect.

So here I am, starting off in a new restaurant, making a new beginning, taking on a new challenge. It's exciting and I want to do it well, but I don't think my ambitions have really changed. Maybe if I were twenty-one again, maybe if things were different, maybe then I'd be looking for my Michelin star. But today I'm not. I want to do what I think I did at Soho Soho and I hope I carry on doing here. My ideal is simple: that people enjoy the food and hopefully come back and I'll just slip out the back door and go home and that's it. That's good enough for me.